U-BOATS
VS
DESTROYER ESCORTS
The Battle of the Atlantic

GORDON WILLIAMSON

First published in Great Britain in 2007 by Osprey Publishing,
Midland House, West Way, Botley, Oxford OX2 0PH, UK
443 Park Avenue South, New York, NY 10016, USA

E-mail: info@ospreypublishing.com

A CIP catalogue record for this book is available from the British Library

ISBN: 978 1 84603 133 5

Page layout by Myriam Bell
Index by Alan Thatcher
Typeset in ITC Conduit and Adobe Garamond
Maps by Boundford.com, Huntingdon. UK
Battlescene painting by Howard Gerrard
Digital artwork by Lee Ray
Originated by PDQ Digital Media Solutions
Printed in China through Bookbuilders

07 08 09 10 11   10 9 8 7 6 5 4 3 2 1

For a catalogue of all books published by Osprey Military and Aviation please contact:

NORTH AMERICA
Osprey Direct, c/o Random House Distribution Center, 400 Hahn Road,
Westminster, MD 21157

E-mail: info@ospreydirect.com

ALL OTHER REGIONS
Osprey Direct UK, P.O. Box 140 Wellingborough, Northants, NN8 2FA, UK

E-mail: info@ospreydirect.co.uk

www.ospreypublishing.com

Artist's note

Readers may care to note that the original painting fr
which the battlescene colour plate in this book was
prepared is available for private sale. All reproduction
copyright whatsoever is retained by the Publishers.
All enquiries should be addressed to:

Howard Gerrard
11 Oaks Road
Tenterden
Kent
TN30 6RD

The Publishers regret that they can enter into no
correspondence upon this matter.

CONTENTS

INTRODUCTION

The battle of the Atlantic pitted Germany's U-boats against Allied convoys sailing from North America and the South Atlantic. The name itself is a bit of a misnomer as it was not one single battle but the longest continuous military campaign of World War II, lasting for six years, stretching over hundreds of miles and involving almost countless combat engagements. By the end of hostilities, the Kriegsmarine's U-boats had sunk in excess of 2,900 ships, representing over 12 million tons of Allied shipping.

Despite some post-war claims that the U-boat campaign had no real chance of being successful in the long run, it is clear that the Allied leaders at the time had a different view. By January 1943, such were the worries over the U-boat's successes that at the Casablanca conference, it was agreed that the defeat of the U-boats was to be a number one priority.

Indeed, when summarizing his thoughts on the Battle of the Atlantic, Prime Minister Winston Churchill famously said, 'The only thing that ever really frightened me during the war was the U-boat peril'.

The Battle of the Atlantic was not only a fight for the survival of Great Britain, but for the survival of real opposition to Hitler. If the U-boat campaign had succeeded and Britain had been starved into subjugation, the British Isles wouldn't have served as a base for the eventual bombing offensive and as a launching point for the invasion of Europe. It is difficult to envisage how the stakes could have been higher.

With the U-boat, the Germans seemed to be in possession of the most lethal and effective of weapons. It was certainly a most formidable foe, developing through the war from a small coastal vessel to a large ocean-going, state-of-the-art, killing machine, the most advanced models produced towards the end of the war having tremendous influence on post-war submarine design. Certainly in the opening months of the war

Leaning against a depth charge thrower, the quarterdeck lookout on board HMS *Viscount* searches the sea for submarines through a pair of binoculars. Some of the ships being convoyed can be seen in the distance. (IWM A13362)

the U-boats stalked the high seas picking off vessels, ranging from small unescorted coastal merchants to heavily protected battleships, seemingly at will.

A similar situation has existed in World War I and the Allies knew that the most effective means of protection was the convoy system, whereby vessels sought safety by sailing in numbers. However, this alone could not sufficiently reduce the number of U-boat kills to secure the vital supply lines and keep Britain in the war.

It was not until the advent of specialized anti-submarine escort types equipped with Radar and ASDIC (the Allies' underwater detection system), and the development of dedicated anti-submarine tactics that there would be an effective answer to the U-boat peril.

Initially the Allies relied on a variety of vessels to protect the convoys and increasingly hunt out the U-boats themselves. These ranged from vintage World War I destroyers to converted civilian whalers. However, the Destroyer Escort (DE) was the first true, purpose-built escort vessel and the duel between these two deadly opponents would be at the heart of the battle.

Over 141 Allied escort vessels paid the ultimate price in their attempts to protect the crucial convoys. In return for their own losses, the Allies would sink nearly 800 U-boats. Over 30,000 of the 39,000 German sailors who served in U-boats would never return – the highest casualty rate of any branch of any armed forces in modern history.

This book describes the design and development of the U-boat, Destroyer Escort and other key escort vessels, analyzing their strengths and weaknesses and assessing their tactics, weaponry and training. Moreover, it is an insight into the lives of the Royal Navy, United States Navy and U-boat crews as they played their deadly games of cat and mouse on the high seas as they gambled not only with their lives but with the fate of the war.

CHRONOLOGY

1935

27 Sept The founding of the first U-boat flotilla of the Kriegsmarine, Unterseebootsflotille Weddigen.

1936

1 Jan Kapitän zur See Karl Dönitz appointed as Führer der Unterseeboote.

1939

Sept The first major success of the U-boat War as Gunther Prien's U-47 penetrates Scapa Flow and sinks the battleship *Royal Oak*.

14 Sept The first U-boat to be destroyed by escorts, U-39, is lost after a failed attack on the aircraft carrier *Ark Royal*.

13 Oct U-42 becomes the first U-boat to be destroyed by escorts during an attack on merchant shipping.

1940

25 Feb The first loss of a U-boat to an Allied surface warship as U-63 is depth charged and sunk by escorts *Inglefield*, *Imogen* and *Escort*. (Two previous kills, against U-36 and U-51 had been achieved by British submarines).

22 June Fall of France gives the U-boats access to Atlantic bases.

July–Aug The first so-called 'Happy Time' for U-Boats with over 200 merchant ships sunk.

16–19 Oct The battle for convoy SC 7 which saw the convoy attacked by seven U-boats and over 79,500 tons of shipping sunk.

A convoy assembles off the east coast of the USA in preparation for the hazardous trip across the Atlantic. When near to land, convoys were often protected by anti-submarine airships, known as "Blimps". (National Archives)

Admiral Ernst J. King. King's Anglophobia resulted in his refusal to accept British advice on the use of the convoy system and resulted in heavy losses to US shipping off the east coast of America in the period immediately after the US entered the war. (Naval Historical Collection)

U-boat ace Kapitänleutnant Gunther Prien, the first of the great aces to be lost in action, during the attack on Convoy OB 293, by which time he had already added the Oakleaves to the Knight's Cross awarded for the sinking of the *Royal Oak* at Scapa Flow in October 1939. (Author's collection)

1941

7 Mar	Gunther Prien becomes the first of the great U-boat aces to be lost in action during an attack on an Allied convoy.
17 Mar	U-100 becomes the first U-boat to be destroyed after detection by ship-borne radar aboard HMS *Vanoc*.
9 May	U-110 captured along with its naval codes and Enigma machine.
27 May	The first convoy (HX 129) to be escorted all the way across the Atlantic.

1942

Jan–Mar	The second 'Happy Time' with over 200 ships sunk off the US coast during Operation *Drumbeat*.
April	USA introduces the convoy system.

June	The most costly convoy battle of the war, with 24 ships from convoy PQ 17, representing well over 140,000 tons sunk.

1943

16–17 Mar	Convoys HX 229 and SC 122 attacked by as many as 20 U-boats, which sink 22 ships totalling 146,000.
24 May	The tide turns as 43 U-Boats are lost for the sinking of just 34 Allied ships. Dönitz ceases U-boat operations in the North Atlantic.
June	Allied merchant shipping construction begins to exceed losses.

1945

25 Feb	The first successful attack on Allied shipping by the new Type XXIII 'electro-boat'.

THE STRATEGIC SITUATION

World War II did not herald the first use of the submarine in combat. Indeed, during World War I, the U-boats of the the Kaiserliche Marine had wrought havoc on Allied shipping. There were a number of U-boat aces, commanders who were responsible for the sinking of several thousand tons of enemy shipping.

After some stunning successes in the opening years of the war, in early 1917 Germany recommenced unrestricted submarine warfare against Allied shipping. With the bulk of the navy's suitable escort vessels allocated to the British Grand Fleet, little was available to protect merchant shipping, and the U-boats initially hit merchant shipping hard. However, the United States made destroyers available to supplement British warships and from April 1917 Lloyd George ordered that all ships carrying much-needed food and provisions to Britain were to sail in convoys as a means of protection.

Merchant shipping losses rapidly declined to acceptable levels and the U-boat menace was gradually neutralized. Without the development of this anti-submarine strategy as well as the support of the United States (a pattern that was repeated in the next world war), this destruction of Allied shipping had come perilously close to bringing Britain to her knees. As a result, the terms of the Versailles Treaty that Germany was forced to accept in 1919 had quite deliberately decimated the German Fleet. Germany's total armed forces strength was not to exceed 100,000 and within that total the navy was not to comprise more than 15,000 men. It was to have just six elderly battleships, six cruisers and 12 destroyers, with submarines totally prohibited. Those U-boats that had survived the war were either seized by the Allies or scrapped.

In view of the damage done by U-boats in World War I, the terms of the subsequent Anglo-German Naval Agreement which was signed on 18 June 1935 were somewhat surprising. This was a considerable coup for Germany, allowing the Germans to increase the size of the Reichsmarine to 35 percent of the size of the Royal Navy. More importantly, it allowed Germany to build submarines once again, up to 45 percent of the Royal Navy's submarine strength.

The relative section of the agreement stated,

> In the matter of submarines, however, Germany, while not exceeding the ratio of 35:100 in respect of total tonnage, shall have the right to possess a submarine tonnage equal to the total submarine tonnage possessed by the Members of the British Commonwealth of Nations. The German Government, however, undertake that, except in the circumstances indicated in the immediately following sentence, Germany's submarine tonnage shall not exceed 45 percent of the total of that possessed by the Members of the British Commonwealth of Nations. The German Government reserve the right, in the event of a situation arising which in their opinion makes it necessary for Germany to avail herself of her right to a percentage of submarine tonnage exceeding the 45 percent abovementioned, to give notice to this effect to His Majesty's Government in the United Kingdom and agree that the matter shall be the subject of friendly discussion before the German Government exercise that right.

Grossadmiral Karl Dönitz, commander-in-chief submarine and eventual commander-in-chief of the navy. Note that on his tunic (top and bottom of the vertical row of badges) are the U-boat War Badges of both world wars. (Author's collection)

To command this new U-boat force, the Kriegsmarine turned to Kapitän zur See Karl Dönitz. Dönitz was born in Grünau near Berlin, joining the Kaiserliche Marine, in 1910. On 27 September 1913, Dönitz was commissioned Leutnant zur See and when war broke out in 1914, served on the cruiser SMS *Breslau*, operating in the Mediterranean and Black Sea. In August 1914, *Breslau* was transferred to the Ottoman navy but retained her German crew, who now wore the Fez as their duty headdress! When the *Breslau* was put into dock for repairs, Dönitz, now an Oberleutnant zur See, was temporarily assigned as an airfield commander. Unhappy with this job, Dönitz applied for transfer to the U-boat service and completed his transfer in October 1916.

Dönitz first served as watch officer on U-39 before gaining his own command – the UC-25 – in February 1918. On 5 September 1918 he took command of UB-68, then operating in the Mediterranean. After a night surface attack on a convoy on the night of 4 October 1918, in the early morning hours of the next day a second, submerged, attack was launched. Due to a technical malfunction, control of the boat was lost and it was forced to the surface.

Dönitz was forced to scuttle his boat but was rescued along with his crew. He remained a prisoner of war of the British until 1919, and in 1920 returned to Germany. His naval career continued and he was promoted to Kapitänleutnant zur See in January 1921. In the new Reichsmarine, the naval arm of the Weimar Republic, he commanded Torpedo boats and became Korvettenkapitän in November 1928.

On 1 September 1933, Dönitz became Fregattenkapitän, and in 1934 took command of the cruiser *Emden*, which he took on a year-long world cruise with a crew of cadets to prepare them for future careers as naval officers. The ship returned to Wilhelmshaven, Germany in July 1935, and in September Dönitz was promoted to *Kapitän zur See* in the new Kriegsmarine. Dönitz was placed in command of the first U-boat flotilla *Weddigen*, at that time comprising just three boats, as *Führer der Unterseeboote*, or F.d.U, a post later renamed as *Befehlshaber der U-Boote* or B.d.U (Commander U-boats). The U-boat arm had been reborn!

Despite the Allies' knowledge of the effectiveness of submarines against merchant shipping, the terms of the Anglo-German Naval Agreement meant that Germany was now in a position to legitimately build a new U-boat force. These new U-boats were to wreak considerable havoc in the early stages of World War II against unescorted merchantmen sailing independently until sufficient escorts were available to allow the convoy system to be reintroduced.

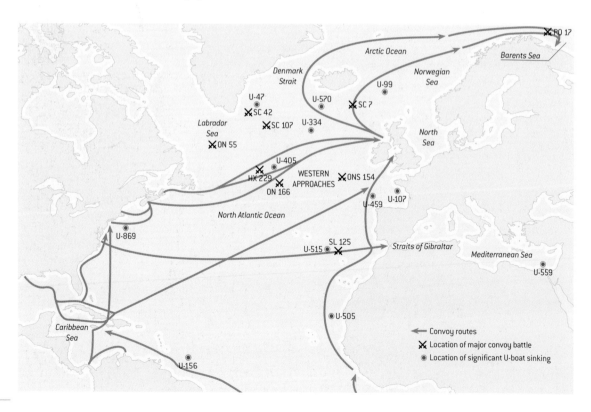

In order to sustain the British economy and feed its population, it was estimated that somewhere in the region of four million tons of supplies per month would be required for the nation's survival. To achieve this a merchant fleet of around 3,000 ships would be required to make those deliveries. This would not be sustainable in the face of concerted U-boat attacks.

At the outbreak of war, Hitler had ordered that his submarines adhere to the so-called *Prize Ordinance*, rule 74 of which stated that a submarine must provide the crew and passengers of a merchant ship with a 'place of safety', before sinking the vessel or taking her as a prize. The lifeboat was not legally considered a "place of safety" unless sea conditions were very calm and the incident was taking place within close range of dry land (from whence the submarine might be attacked) or another ship, which could take them on board (and might equally decide to attempt to ram the submarine). This of course put the submarine at a considerable disadvantage as many of these rules would be almost impossible to meet in most circumstances.

MERCHANT SEAMEN

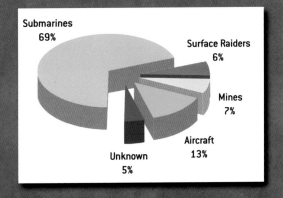

Over 30,000 seamen from the British merchant navy were lost between 1939 and 1945 and thousands more from the American and other Allied merchant navies. One in 26 US mariners serving aboard merchant vessels in World War II died in the frontline of duty, suffering a greater percentage of war-related deaths than all other US services. Theirs was a constantly fought battle with no respite. Even during the so-called 'Phoney War' between September 1939 and May 1940, 177 British merchant ships were lost, and for almost six years afterwards barely a day went by without the loss of merchant ships and their civilian crews. In total, approximately 12 million tons of merchant shipping was lost during the Battle of the Atlantic. Great secrecy surrounded the deployment of convoys and the crews and their families were constantly reminded of the importance of this. At the time the high casualty rate was kept secret to attract and keep mariners at sea. This possibly contributed to the lack of public recognition merchant mariners received post-war for their valiant service. Nonetheless, the dangers they faced were acknowledged by the Allied servicemen drafted to protect them, in the words of one: 'Those of us who have escorted convoys in either of the great wars can never forget the days and especially the nights spent in company with those slow-moving squadrons of iron tramps – the wisps of smoke from their funnels, the phosphorescent wakes, the metallic clang of iron doors at the end of the night watches which told us that the Merchant Service firemen were coming up after four hours in the heated engine rooms, or boiler rooms, where they had run the gauntlet of torpedoes or mines for perhaps half the years of the war. I remember so often thinking that those in the engine rooms, if they were torpedoed, would probably be drowned before they reached the engine room steps...'

This chart shows the principal causes of damage to Allied merchant shipping. Contrary to the pre-war belief of both German and British naval leaders, the surface ship played only a small role in inflicting damage against Allied merchant ships; the submarine was by far the greatest menace.

With several Wrens standing around it, the 'Table' is laid out on the floor for a class at the Western Approaches Tactical School, Derby House, Liverpool. Here naval officers were taught the strategy of anti-U-boat warfare. (IWM A009891)

It should be noted that many U-boat commanders indeed attempted to follow these rules, often giving food, water and directions to the nearest land, to the crews of ships which had been given time to take to their lifeboats.

However, on 23 September these rules were relaxed in the case of any enemy ship which attempted to use its radio to summon aid. By the end of that month, any enemy vessels encountered within the area of the North Sea were also declared fair game. Further relaxations followed, including the end of the prohibition on attacking liners, as it was considered that these were often used as troopships and were therefore deemed viable targets.

U-boats during this period tended to act alone (partly of course due to the small number actually available at sea at any one time) though once enemy ships had been spotted and their presence reported to B.d.U, other U-boats would be vectored in to the same position to join the attack. Actual Wolfpack tactics, with a number of boats acting in co-ordinated groups from the outset, did not come into general use until 1941. Dönitz had first used the term *Rudel* to describe this strategy of submarine warfare. *Rudel* translates best as 'pack of animals' and became known in English as a 'Wolfpack'.

During the closing months of 1939, some half a million tons of shipping had been sunk by U-boats for the loss of just nine of their own. The fall of France in 1940 gave the U-Bootwaffe a massive boost. Of the 57 boats Dönitz had at his disposal, only 27 were ocean-going. Until the fall of France, the range of the U-boats had been constrained geographically; access to the Atlantic convoy routes necessitated long and risky journeys from the northern German ports around the north of Scotland. With the acquisition of the French Atlantic ports, Dönitz could take advantage of the increased dockyard capacity and proximity to the convoy-lanes which enabled him to expand operations into the central and western Atlantic. Previously abritrary and sporadic U-boat actions were transformed into more regular and consistent attacks on convoys. U-boat bases were quickly established at Brest, Lorient, Bordeaux, La Rochelle, La Pallice and St. Nazaire. Their immediate success following the establishment of these bases was termed the 'Happy Times' with the U-boats sinking over 200 merchant ships between July and August.

Overall 1940 was a successful year for Dönitz. Although British coastal defences had been toughened up, making life difficult for the small Type II coastal boats, the bigger types operating in the Atlantic achieved considerable successes. From the summer of 1940 through to the end of that year, well over 1.6 million tons of merchant shipping was sunk. This was not gained without cost, however, as 25 U-boats were lost during that year. The balance, nevertheless, was still very much in favour of the Germans, as with 54 new boats being launched, German production was still exceeding its losses. If the U-boats could continue to sink Allied merchant shipping at this rate, faster than Great Britain could build replacements, the prospects for the British were bleak.

However, by 1941 the reintroduction of the convoy system and the availability of more and more escort vessels, armed with ASDIC and Radar saw the rate of German successes begin to falter. The entry of the United States into the war with

Bearded after a long war cruise, and with his tunic adorned with flowers to celebrate his safe return, here we see Wolfgang Lüth, one of only two U-boat commanders to win the coveted Knight's Cross with Oakleaves, Swords and Diamonds. (Author's collection)

the vast construction potential of that nation not only for warships but also merchantmen, would see the beginning of the end of any hopes of victory for the U-boats, although the lack of anti-submarine warfare experience of the United States initially saw the U-boats score tremendous successes off the US coast during the second of the so-called 'Happy Times'. The USA had considered convoys as being too 'passive' a method of defence with an offensive plan to use warships to hunt the U-boats being preferred. This policy led to disaster. In the first six months of 1942 alone, over 200 ships were sunk in US coastal waters by around 20 U-boats. The US learnt its lesson the hard way and introduced the convoy system. From then onwards the U-boats would be engage in a literal fight to the death with Allied escort forces.

Throughout the course of the war a myriad of different ship types would be involved in the battle against the U-boats. In many cases this was brought about by sheer necessity, with vessels that were often far from ideal for this type of warfare being pressed into service. Many, such as the destroyer, fulfilled this task admirably, but these warships were intended for service with the fleet, in warship versus warship actions. The requirement for a vessel which was purpose-built to protect merchant convoys against submarines as well as secure U-boat 'kills' would eventually result in the emergence of a new class of vessel, the Destroyer Escort. This was strictly speaking, a US Navy term, and these warships were generally known as frigates within the Royal Navy.

These vessels were the forerunners of today's modern anti-submarine warships whose modest size belie their destructive power. In subsequent years frigates and destroyers would comprise the bulk of most navy's surface fleets, with only aircraft carriers from amongst the largest surface ships surviving into the 21st century.

DESIGN AND DEVELOPMENT

THE U-BOAT

Following the end of World War I, the prohibition on Germany possessing submarines could have had a devastating effect on German ability to develop new designs. However, this problem was neatly avoided by Germany continuing to assist in the design of submarines for other nations. A cover firm, the Ingenieurskanntor voor Scheepsbouw (IvS) was set up in Holland, but this apparently neutral, commercial firm was in fact funded and controlled by the Reichsmarine. Submarines were designed for a number of countries including Argentina, Spain, Finland and Turkey so that, when in 1932, Germany decided to embark on a naval reconstruction programme, a number of designs were available which could be quickly adapted for German naval use.

Germany's pre-war U-boat construction programme envisaged the following types being built:

1934   2 large 800-ton boats and two small 250-ton boats
1935   4 small 250-ton boats
1936   2 large 800-ton boats and 6 small 250-ton boats
1937   2 large 800-ton boats and 6 small 250-ton boats

The terms of the Anglo-German Naval Agreement of 1935 would in principle have allowed a fleet totalling around 17,500 tons. This was initially perceived as being 20 of the larger type and six of the smaller. However, pervailing naval thinking

View from the "Wintergarden" platform as it is passed by a fellow Type VII in heavy seas. (Author's collection)

considered a larger number of the smaller type as more effective than a smaller number of the large boats. At this time a war with the USA was not considered likely and the need for larger boats able to operate far out into the Atlantic was not anticipated, hence the concentration on small to medium submarines for potential use against the perceived likely enemy, Great Britain. A figure of around ten of the larger boats and 18 of the smaller was arrived at, still leaving Germany well within her theoretical tonnage allowance.

German submarine design followed a logical progression in numbering, each new design being allocated the next type number, always expressed in Roman numerals. The first submarine to be put into production was the Type I. Construction of two boats began in June 1935 at the AG Weser yard in Bremen, with the finished boats commissioned in April and May 1936. Only two were ever built, though the reasons for this seem to be mired in political interference rather than any inherent faults in the boats themselves. Despite the fact that they were considered to be somewhat difficult to handle with poor stability and slow diving speeds, they were still effective weapons. Although the two boats had a relatively short combat career of less than one year – both being sunk in the summer of 1940 – between them they sunk 18 enemy ships.

The Type II, a small offshore vessel intended primarily for action in the coastal waters around the British Isles, was the first type to be constructed in significant numbers and was based on an IvS design for Finland. A total of 50 were produced, in four sub-variants Type IIA to Type IID. Many had already been relegated to training duties by the outbreak of war and had to be recalled for frontline service due to the shortage of operational boats. They accounted for over 200 enemy ships sunk, including several surface warships.

Type numbers III to VI were allocated to design projects which never got off the drawing board so that the next submarine to enter production was the Type VII, the boat which would become the mainstay of the U-Bootwaffe throughout the war.

The Type VII was the brainchild of Dr Friedrich Schürer and Ministerialdirigent Fritz Bröking, two of the top officials of the Naval Construction Office. Schürer's contribution to U-boat development was recognized by the naming of a U-boat in the West German Navy in his honour in 1966. The Type VII's far greater endurance, greater payload capacity, inherent robustness and relatively fast dive speed would serve the Kriegsmarine well and the Type VII would become the boat in which the greatest of the U-boat aces would score their most impressive successes.

With the fall of France and German acquisition of bases giving them direct access to the Atlantic, Type VII boats would be able to strike right across to American waters and with U-boat Tanker support allowing longer operational deployment times, no part of the North or South Atlantic would be safe from the U-boats.

A total of six principal variants were produced, Type VIIA through to Type VIIF. All of the Type A boats had been lost or relegated to training duties before the Battle of the Atlantic, the main protagonist in which would be the Type VIIB and VIIC. A total of just over 700 Type VII boats were produced by the end of the war. Still relatively small – certainly in comparison with US submarine types, it was extremely congested and life on board was never luxurious. Its fast diving speed in the hands of a well-trained crew and the fact that on many occasions it was proved that these boats were able to dive well below the shipyard recommended maximum safe depth of around 100m and even the theoretical crush depth of 200m to evade the enemy and emerge unscathed, meant that they were popular types with the crews. Around 2,600 war cruises were undertaken by Type VII boats in the course of which some 1,365 enemy ships were sunk.

The U-boat commander had to remain stationary at his post as there was so little space within the conning tower. Rotation of the periscope was controlled by depressing pedals with the feet. Additionally the left hand controlled the height of the periscope, the right angle of the upper prism, giving the commander a possible field of view between 15 degrees below the horizon to 70 above. (Royal Navy Submarine Museum)

The last major U-boat type to feature in the Battle of the Atlantic was the Type IX, the proposed Type VIII design never progressing beyond design stages. The Type IX was designed and developed due to the perceived requirement for a boat which could easily operate far out into the South Atlantic, along the African coast and into the Mediterranean, without the type of refuelling support that the Type VII required. In the event, Type IXs would eventually range even farther afield, operating into the Indian and Pacific Oceans.

Its great range, and its capability of carrying 24 torpedoes instead of the average 14 of a Type VII made it a formidable weapon. However, its large size made it a slower boat to dive and, despite its greater roominess meaning that the crews had slightly

Keeping a U-boat in fighting trim required constant ministrations from the boat's technical crew. While seamen aboard kept four-hour duty watches, the engineers maintained six-hour shifts. Here, as the boat moves underwater on electric motors, Maschinenobergfreiter Walter Labahn on-board U-564 works on changing a cylinder head of the engine under his responsibility assisted by the Diesel Obermaschinist Hermann Krahn, in his effort to loosen the holding nuts on the cylinder head. (Royal Navy Submarine Museum)

less discomfort than those on the Type VIIs, many U-boat men felt safer on the Type VIIs because the faster dive speed allowed them a better chance to evade the enemy if caught on the surface.

Of the 194 Type IX U-boats built in four main variants Type IXA to IXD, only 24 survived the end of hostilities – a higher loss rate than that suffered by the Type VIIs.

Throughout the war, improvements were made both to the Type VII and Type IX boats but these were basically stop-gap measures whilst development of the new Type XXI and Type XXIII 'Electro-Boats' proceeded. Both heavily influenced post-war submarine design, and were the first boats to have such massive battery power, treble that of a Type VII, that their underwater speed was actually faster than their surface speed, which well exceeded the speeds some escorts could reach. Earlier U-boats had far less battery capacity, with the result that once under water and running on electric motors, their maximum speeds and endurance were severely limited.

The Type XXI and Type XXIII boats, although technically far in advance of anything the Allies possessed, did not make it into operational service in sufficient numbers to affect the course of the war. Only a handful of ships were sunk by Type XXIIIs in the closing days of the war and none by Type XXIs.

THE ESCORTS

The combined number of different classes/types of escort used in the war against the U-boats, when taking all the Allied nations into account, was vast, and would require far more space than is available here to cover in depth. This section will therefore deal with the principal generic types used by the main protagonists, the Royal Navy and United States Navy, in particular the Destroyer Escorts (also designated as frigates) that

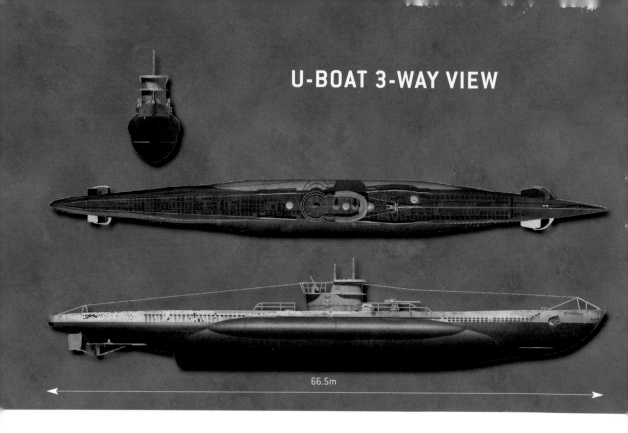

U-BOAT 3-WAY VIEW

66.5m

Shown here is a typical Type VIIC U-boat. The saddle tanks and areas of the hull below the waterline were painted a very dark grey with the upper works a pale grey. As shown here, the U-boat's paintwork would rapidly become weathered and rusted during the Atlantic operations and boats returning from a long patrol would often look decidedly shabby. Later U-boats lost the forward deck gun and gained heavier anti-aircraft armament on the conning tower platforms.

were the only kind of vessel specifically designed and developed to tackle the U-boat itself as well as undertaking the primary task of protecting the convoy.

The general convoy system arranged the merchant ships in a 'box' formation of columns, with four ships per column in as many as ten columns. The most strategically important ships carrying cargoes such as petroleum and other vital cargoes were positioned in the relative safety of the centre of the convoy. Less important cargoes were positioned on the outskirts of the convoy and were the most likely first targets for any approaching U-boat.

A typical convoy escort of six, would see the escort commander in a destroyer, supported by five smaller escorts – including frigates/DEs as well as other vessels. The destroyer would position itself ahead of the convoy during daylight (and move to the rear at night). The remaining escorts would take up positions at port and starboard at the head of the convoy, at port and starboard around the centre flank of the convoy with one escort bringing up the rear.

The fast speed of the destroyer would allow it to race ahead on detecting and potentially intercepting a U-boat before it could reach the merchants. If a U-boat succeeded in penetrating the escort screen the slower-moving, but far more manoeuvrable DEs and corvettes, could weave in and out of the convoy columns pursuing the slow moving submarine.

Although destroyers played an invaluable part in convoy defence, it was a case of 'making do' with warships being pressed into service on work for which they were not ideally suited. The frigate/DE which evolved during the Battle of the Atlantic was the first warship ideally suited to anti-submarine work, adapting and refining the best features of the corvettes and sloops which preceded it.

It is interesting to note that as far as classification is concerned it is said that the term Destroyer Escort (DE) came to be used by the US Navy because of the anglophobic Admiral King who refused to allow the British terminology of frigate to be used for US warships. The modern US Navy has now adopted the internationally used term of frigate for those ships once classed as DEs.

ROYAL NAVY

As war loomed, the bulk of the navy's smaller warship strength lay in its destroyer fleet, many of which were rather elderly. Of course it could not at that time have been foreseen that Germany would quickly conquer France and acquire Atlantic sea ports, so the British could be forgiven for thinking that it had adequate resources to bottle up any German submarines between the extensive minefields in the Channel and the heavy British naval presence in the North Sea, preventing German vessels escaping into the Atlantic through the waters around the north of the British Isles.

Within weeks of the outbreak of war, U-47 had penetrated one of the Royal Navy's most important bases at Scapa Flow and had sunk the battleship HMS *Royal Oak*. It had been brought home to the British in no uncertain fashion, that the U-boat menace that had threatened Britain's survival in World War I was back, and warships suited to anti-submarine warfare would be needed urgently.

Destroyers were expensive to produce and were effectively choice, if dangerous, targets in their own right. What was needed was a vessel that was cheap to produce, needed only the kind of machinery required to allow it to outrun existing submarine types, and with specialized armament for anti-submarine warfare (ASW) rather than against other surface ships.

Two existing types available at the start of the war were used predominantly for anti-submarine escort duties, these being the elderly V and W classes of destroyers. Despite being designs which were introduced before the end of World War I, they gave sterling service as anti-submarine escorts.

The V and W classes displaced around 1,100 tons and were crewed by just over 130 officers and men. Initially, they were armed with two triple torpedo tubes, and carried four 4-in. guns in single gun turrets, but this armament was altered when they were re-designated Escort Destroyers as opposed to Fleet Destroyers. The V and W destroyers were an amalgam of six similar classes of destroyers built for the Royal Navy under the War Emergency Programme of World War I and are generally classed under one umbrella designation. For their time they were considered the most powerful and advanced ships of their time. The destroyers were originally designed to support the Grand Fleet in its actions in the North Sea, for which they had been required to make fairly short, high-speed dashes. Thus they were unsuitable for the ocean escort role to which they found themsleves allocated in World War II, where speeds of over 20 knots were of limited value and endurance was just as desirable as firepower. To remedy such shortcomings, adaptations were made to suit them to this new sort of warfare. The small single-unit boiler room was struck and the resulting space divided into fuel tanks (lower) and accommodation (upper). Not only did this lower fuel consumption but

The Buckley Class Destroyer Escort USS *Fiske* (DE 143). This class was well armed with medium and light artillery, Hedgehog mortars and depth charges. (Naval Historical Collection)

it also increased bunkerage, providing much needed space for ballooning wartime crews. The powerful anti-warship 'A' and 'Y' guns were landed and replaced with a Hedgehog weapon throwing mechanism as well as depth-charge stowage and launchers.

Further modifications were made dependent on the kind of convoy escort duties they were to perform. For duties as fast escorts, 16 of these destroyers also had their torpedo tubes removed and main armament altered to two twin 4-in. gun turrets. Top speed was 34 knots. For duties as long-range escorts 22 examples were converted, also losing their torpedo tubes and having their main armament reduced to two 4-in. guns. The reduction in weight allowed them to carry far more fuel to increase their range but resulted in a reduction in top speed to 25 knots. This, however, was still far more than was needed to escort slow-moving convoys and outpace any U-boat.

The need for some additional escort vessels was recognized almost immediately the war began, but it was envisaged that the need would only be for the protection of British coastal waters. This resulted in the creation of the Flower Class corvette, a design based on that of a civilian whaler, with shallow draft for operating in inshore waters. These ships were slow and lightly armed, but performed extremely well. A class of 267 corvettes was developed by the Royal Navy and Royal Canadian Navy. They were initially perceived as stop-gap measure against the U-boats because they could be developed quickly and easily. Their simple design used parts that were commonly found in merchant vessels, which meant that they could be constructed at small commercial shipyards all over the UK and eastern Canada, where the larger vessels like destroyers could not be built. There was also an additional advantage in that the largely reserve and volunteer crews who manned the corvettes were familiar with their operation. As a result the corvettes were crucial to convoy protection in the first half of the war.

With the rapid fall of France meaning that the U-Bootwaffe could operate well out into the Atlantic, threatening Allied merchant shipping from the US, Canada and elsewhere, it became necessary for these little corvettes to operate in the ferocious waters of the Atlantic where, though they could withstand the punishment, they would be tossed around mercilessly, pitching and rolling and making life on board

extremely unpleasant. The fact that these vessels could be developed quickly and easily made them the perfect stop-gap measure against the U-boats, but a long-term solution was still required.

The first serious convoy escort warships for the Royal Navy in World War II were the Black Swan Class sloops. These were purpose-built escort vessels, although they were in fact dual purpose and intended to provide not only anti-submarine cover but also anti-aircraft cover. They were designed to have a longer range than a destroyer at the expense of a lower top speed, while remaining capable of outrunning surfaced Type VII and Type IX boats.

A total of 37 were produced, and although not a purely anti-submarine weapon, they did succeed in destroying 29 U-boats – however, four were sunk by the submarines they hunted. Ironically, a number were transferred to the West German Navy after the war. Although a handful were built early in the war, the bulk of the Black Swans were constructed between 1943 and 1945.

It was with the arrival of the River Class frigates, designed by naval engineer William Reid, that the British finally had a superb purpose-built and designed Anti-Submarine Warfare (ASW) vessel. The first appeared in late 1941 and a total of 151 were ultimately built. These ships fulfilled all the needs of a first-class escort. They were specifically designed for and could withstand the rigours of service in the North Atlantic, were fast to build, had a far greater range than corvettes and sloops, were relatively cheap (meaning, in cost terms, they were expendable unlike a very costly destroyer) and were laden with highly effective ASW weaponry. The excellent sea-keeping qualities of this design also made it a much more comfortable ship for its crews than the smaller corvettes and sloops. The majority served with the Royal Navy and Royal Canadian Navy but others also served with the Royal Australian and Free French, while ten Canadian-built ships were assigned to the US Navy. The

The American-built Captain Class frigates (acquired under the Lend-Lease scheme) HMS *Berry*, HMS *Duckworth* and HMS *Essington*, seen in Plymouth harbour after returning from convoy escort duty. (IWM A023465)

River Class was designed to correct all the perceived flaws in the Flower Class and the most significant improvements related to the greater size, range and speed. It was such a particularly flexible design that it became the direct predecessor of today's modern frigates. The design was sufficiently impressive that it was copied by the US Navy where it became the Tacoma Class Destroyer Escort.

A modified version of the River Class hull, using pre-fabrication methods, improved radar and armed with two triple-barrelled anti-submarine mortars in place of the Hedgehog, was further developed to produce the Loch Class, with 28 examples seeing service from 1944 onwards. One of these, *Loch Killin*, sank U-333, the U-boat formerly commanded by ace Peter "Ali" Cremer. Cremer had passed the U-boat over to a new commander just 12 days earlier. U-333 went to the bottom with all hands.

The combination of destroyers, corvettes, sloops and frigates served the Royal Navy well during the Battle of the Atlantic.

In addition, a number of aging US Navy 'Four Stacker' destroyers, so named because of their four funnels, were supplied to Great Britain under the Lend-Lease programme. No longer suited for combat roles against other modern surface warships they did well in the anti-submarine role. The US also supplied a number of Buckley Class DEs which had been built to British specification and which served in the Royal Navy as Captain Class frigates.

UNITED STATES NAVY

Despite having the largest destroyer fleet in the World at the end of World War I, the USA had either decommissioned or scrapped over 240 of these vessels by 1934 without a single new destroyer being launched. However, by the second half of the 1930s the rebirth of Germany as a military power had encouraged new destroyer construction in the USA, with over 40 new destroyers being launched. By the summer of 1940 the destroyers of the Atlantic Squadron of the US Fleet had their own command.

The US supplied a number of its Buckley Class DEs under Lend-Lease to Great Britain where they were defined as "Captain" Class frigates, named after Napoleonic captains. Here we see HMS *Steckham*. (Imperial War Museum Photograph A-22515)

ESCORT 3-WAY VIEW

114.7m

12m

Prior to the US entry into World War II, although technically neutral, the US Navy had maintained fairly robust anti-submarine patrols off the US coast and had dropped depth charges on suspected U-boats intruding into US-controlled waters.

In October 1941, the USS *Kearney* was torpedoed and damaged by a U-boat whilst providing escort protection to a Canadian convoy, and just two weeks later the USS *Reuben James* became the first US warship to be sunk by the Germans in World War II when she was torpedoed by U-552 whilst escorting a convoy in the waters to the west of Ireland. One month later the USA entered the war.

As with the Royal Navy, destroyers were the largest USN escort vessels, categorized by the USN with the prefix 'DD'. The Wickes and Clemson Classes at 1,000–1,215 tons with four 4-in. guns were the famed elderly four stacker flush-deck destroyers supplied to Great Britain under Lend-Lease and performed sterling service on anti-submarine escort duties.

The Fletcher Class was probably the most successful US destroyer design of all time and took part in many battles with the Kriegsmarine's U-boats. A total of 175 were built, in shipyards all across the USA and many served on well after the end of the war, including some supplied to the West German Navy. The Fletcher hull, in a slightly modified form, was also the basis for the Allen M Sumner Class and Gearing Class variants. The former used the basic Fletcher Class hull but upgraded the main armament, and the latter extended the basic Fletcher Class hull by 4m increasing the fuel bunkerage and thus the operational range.

This illustration shows the layout of a typical Fletcher class destroyer. Note the racks at the stern from which depth charges are rolled into the wake of the warship as well as three depth charge throwers along each side of the aft superstructure. This allowed a 'pattern' of up to eight depth charges to be launched at the same time.

It was not until the British request to the Americans to produce a frigate to their specifications that the US Navy began to build up its own specialized ASW force.

It was the Destroyer which carried the brunt of the US effort against the U-boats for the first part of the war, until the advent of the purpose built DEs.

The British specifications led to the design and construction of the Evarts Class, the first of the new DE classes to appear. The main criteria for the British were the ability to design a warship suitable for operations in the open oceans of the Atlantic and which could be built economically and in great numbers using the mass-production methods for which the USA was renowned.

Effectively the British wanted an equivalent of the River Class frigates, but which could be built faster and cheaper thanks to the vast industrial and shipbuilding capacity of the USA. These ships were pre-fabricated at various factories in the United States and the units brought together in the shipyards where they were welded together on the slipways. In all 32 Evarts Class ships were delivered to the Royal Navy, where they formed part of the Captain Class frigates named after Napoleonic captains.

It was a excellent and successful design, compromised only by its need for four V12 Diesel engines as its powerplant. These engines were also in demand for submarines and landing craft, vessels which were given a higher priority, thus forcing a rethink on how the DEs would be powered. Accordingly, General Electric developed a steam-powered turbo-electric design – the TE type – that would build upon the 12,000 shaft horsepower (shp) and 24 knots of the original DE concept. The resulting design consumed more space than the original geared turbine plant, so the Evarts Class hull was lengthened by 6ft to accommodate it. This resulted in the Buckley Class, its 306ft 'long hull' design becoming the standard hull structure for all later DE classes. Over 150 of the type were commissioned, several serving in the RN as Captain Class frigates alongside the original Buckley Class delivery.

Ultimately, the availability of more diesel engines resulted in the original specification engines of four General Motors diesel engines being placed into the lengthened hull used for the Buckley Class, the new vessel being designated as the Cannon Class.

Two of the most important types of escort vessel during the Battle of the Atlantic were the DEs such as the Edsall Class USS *Huse* shown here which provided sterling service against the U-Boats and the small Escort Carriers, which provided much needed air cover. (Naval Historical Collection).

The Fletcher Class Destroyer USS *Aaron Ward* pictured here in August 1942 carrying one of the more complex camouflage designs on her hull and superstructure. She carried five 5" guns and eight torpedo tubes as well as numerous 20mm cannon and depth charges. (National Archives)

The final modification based on the original Evarts design was the Edsall Class. This once again used the long Buckley Class hull, powered by diesel engines, but in this case the diesels were a Fairbanks Morse design intended for submarine use. All of these Evarts-based variants – the Buckley, Cannon and Edsall – appeared over the space of a few months and bore a striking visual similarity to each other.

One further class of ship which achieved some success against the U-boats whilst serving on convoy escort duties was the US Coastguard cutter, specifically the Treasury Class. Seven of this class had been constructed between 1936 and 1937 for search-and-rescue missions and to interdict drug smugglers. Displacing just over 2,300 tons, they could achieve top speeds of up to 20 knots and had a range of up to 7,000 miles, making them ideal for escort duties. Cheap to build and extremely robust, they were armed with a single 5-in. gun and a number of 40mm and 20mm anti-aircraft guns. These cutters achieved the best kill rate of any type of US escort during World War II.

In addition, the USN possessed a large number of small sub-chasers (SC) of just 98 tons displacement and with a single 3-in. gun for use against submarines operating close to the US coastline. These were not named as such, but merely carried an SC pennant number.

The war against the U-boats during the Battle of the Atlantic was responsible for the emergence of one of the most important types of warship still in existence today, the frigate. Long gone are the days when battleships and cruisers ruled the waves and even the mightiest nuclear-powered aircraft carriers can be despatched by a single torpedo from an enemy submarine. The modern frigate, with its powerful gun and missile armament, and ASW weaponry that World War II servicemen could only have dreamt of, can trace its development back to the frigates and DEs that protected the convoys of World War II from Hitler's U-boats.

TECHNICAL
SPECIFICATIONS

THE U-BOAT

The basic construction of the U-boat consisted of a long tubular pressure hull tapering at each end and divided into watertight compartments. Let into the pressure hull were torpedo tubes (normally four in the bow and either one or two in the stern) and a conning tower which housed the commander's attack position. Around this pressure hull was the outer skin with a free flooding space between the two. The outer skin could absorb considerable damage without affecting the safety of the boat. The pressure hull was also extremely strong, giving the average U-boat the ability to dive safely to far greater depths than most Allied submarine types. If the pressure hull was damaged however, perhaps by enemy gunfire if the U-boat had been caught on the surface, it would effectively be helpless, unable to dive and at the mercy of its foes.

The Type I
Length: 72m
Beam: 6.2m
Displacement: 862 tons surfaced, 983 tons submerged
Powerplant: 2 x 1,540bhp MAN diesel motors with 2 x 500bhp electric motors
Max speed: 17.8 knots surfaced, 8.3 knots submerged

LATER U-BOAT VARIANTS

1. Type IX: This illustrates U-38, an earlier Type IXA model. U-38 was somewhat unusual in sporting a strong camouflage pattern of dark grey blotches over a light grey hull. Having been deployed in the Atlantic, the weathered paintwork reflects the impact the sea and climate would have.

2. This is the superb Type XXI. Unlike most older boats whose maximum speed under water was only half, or even less, of their surfaced speed, the Type XXI could move faster under water than many ships on the surface. This illustration shows U-2511, commanded by Adalbert Schnee and one of only two

Type XXIs that actually carried out a war cruise. Schnee later had the tower of the boat painted white as this was believed to make it less conspicuous from the air.

3. This coastal boat XXII, like the Type XXI, sacrificed external fittings for streamlining. These were excellent boats, though somewhat limited in having only two torpedoes and no reloads. The last U-boat victories of the war were scored by the Type XXII. This shows U-2367, scuttled in 1945 and raised again in 1956 to serve in the West German Navy as the Hecht (Pike).

(Artwork by Ian Palmer © Osprey Publishing)

Complement: 43 officers and men
Armament: 6 torpedo tubes
         1 x 105mm gun
         1 x 20mm gun

The Type II

Length: 40.9m
Beam: 4.1m
Displacement: 254 tons surfaced, 301 tons submerged
Powerplant: 2 x 350bhp MWM diesel motors with 2 x 180bhp electric motors
Max speed: 13 knots surfaced, 6.9 knots submerged
Complement: 25 officers and men
Armament: 3 torpedo tubes
         1 x 20mm gun

The Type VII

Type VIIB

Length: 66.5m
Beam: 6.2m
Displacement: 753 tons surfaced, 857 tons submerged
Powerplant: 2 x 1,400bhp MAN diesel motors with 2 x 375 bhp electric motors
Max speed: 17.2 knots surfaced, 8 knots submerged
Complement: 44 officers and men
Armament: 5 torpedo tubes
         1 x 88mm gun
         1 x 20mm gun

Type VIIC/41

Length: 67.2m
Beam: 6.2m
Displacement: 759 tons surfaced, 860 tons submerged
Powerplant: 2 x 1,400bhp MAN Diesel Motors with 2 x 375bhp Electric Motors
Max speed: 17 knots surfaced, 7.6 knots submerged
Complement: 44 officers and men
Armament: 5 torpedo tubes
         1 x 37mm gun
         2 x Twin 20mm guns

The Type VII that was encountered in the closing stages of the war was a far different vessel to that

Oberleutnant Zur See Ulf Lawaetz and a First Watch crewmate scour the seas as the bow of this Type VIIC forges ahead. Note the heavy rain gear used by U-boat crew, nicknamed 'der Grosse Seehund' (the big Seal). Watches lasted for four hours and were an exhausting but vital task. Before the use of effective radar systems this was the only means of spotting a convoy and/or escort vessels. (Royal Naval Submarine Museum)

in which many U-boat men began the war in 1939. Early versions of the type carried an 88mm gun on the foredeck just ahead of the conning tower with a single 20mm anti-aircraft gun mounted either on the deck to the rear of the tower or on a small circular platform abaft the tower. By the end of the war, the 88mm deck gun had been deleted, few U-boats being willing to risk staying on the surface long enough to be able to use such a weapon. Instead, the area to the rear of the tower was fitted with platforms, generally on two layers and known as the Winter Gardens which carried vastly improved anti-aircraft weaponry, often two twin 20mm guns on the upper platform with either a 37mm anti-aircraft gun or a quadruple 20mm gun on the lower. Despite the added defensive fire power that this extra weaponry provided, and the fact that some U-boats did indeed succeed in shooting down attacking aircraft, the majority of such engagements resulted in the destruction of the U-boat, so that most sensible commanders would opt to dive out of harm's way whenever possible rather than enter combat with enemy aircraft.

The Type IX
Type IXC
Length: 76.8m
Beam: 6.9m
Displacement: 1,144 tons surfaced, 1,257 tons submerged
Powerplant: 2 x 2,200bhp MAN diesel motors with 2 x 500bhp electric motors
Max Speed: 18.3 knots surfaced, 7.3 knots submerged
Complement: 48 officers and men
Armament: 6 torpedo tubes
       1 x 105mm gun
       1 x 37mm gun
       1 x 20mm gun

Excluding for the moment the Type XXI and Type XXIII which were beginning to enter serving as the war ended, the main combat models which served Germany throughout the war – the Type II, Type VII and Type IX boats – were generally smaller than their Allied equivalents. By comparison the US Gato Class was huge, displacing well over 1,500 tons. German submarines were cramped, with limited endurance without refuelling support and limited payload. Nevertheless they were a highly effective weapon, responsible for sinking an incredible 3,000 enemy ships totalling nearly 15 million tons.

Unfortunately for the Third Reich, Allied advances in anti-submarine weaponry outstripped the speed in advances in German submarine development. A combination of the Allied cracking of the German coding system, allowing them to track and trace U-boat movements, and the development of ever more effective anti-submarine weaponry led to the defeat of the U-Bootwaffe rather than any inherent problem with the U-boats themselves, these submarines generally being every bit as good, if not better, than Allied designs.

THE ESCORTS

ROYAL NAVY

V Class destroyer

A total of 75 of the Admiralty V & W Class destroyers were built in the second half of World War I. Well outdated for fleet duty, they still fulfilled a vital role in convoy escort actions. Two of the 16 were converted for use as escorts, including *Vanoc* which, gained fame for its successful anti-submarine actions in the war.

Vanoc as refitted for convoy escort duty.

Length: 91.4m

Beam: 8.15m

Displacement:1,339 tons

Powerplant: Brown Curtis steam turbines

Max Speed: 34 knots

Endurance: 3,500 nautical miles

Detection equipment: Type 286 fixed antenna Radar, ASDIC

Complement: 110 officers and men

Armament: 2 x 4-in guns

        1 x 12 pdr anti-aircraft gun

        4 x 20mm Oerlikon

        Hedgehog mortar

        Depth charges

The elderly but effective W Class destroyer HMS *Walker*, commanded by Commander MacIntyre, was responsible for the sinking of U-99, commanded by top ace Otto Kretschmer during an attack on a convoy in March 1941. (Imperial War Museum Photograph A-4593)

Flower Class corvette

A total of 267 of these small ships were constructed, and used principally by the Royal Navy and the Royal Canadian Navy, though some were also supplied to the US Navy. Much of the machinery used was civilian specification, meaning that crews of former merchant seamen could adapt quickly to serving on board.

Length: 62.5m

Beam: 10m

Displacement: 940 tons

Powerplant: 1 x triple expansion steam engine

Max speed: 16 knots

Endurance: 3,500 nautical miles

Typical detection equipment: Type 271 Radar, ASDIC, HF/DF

Complement: 85 officers and men

Armament: 1 x 4-in. gun

        2 x twin 0.5-in. machine guns

        2 x 0.303-in. machine guns

        Hedgehog mortar

        Depth charges

Black Swan Class sloop

Only 37 ships of this class were completed and served in both the Royal Navy and the Royal Indian Navy. The name-ship of the class, HMS *Black Swan*, was built by Yarrow Shipbuilders and commissioned in January 1940.

Length: 86.25m

Beam: 11.6m

Displacement: 1,350 tons

Powerplant: 2 x 3,600hp steam turbines

Max Speed: 19 knots

Endurance: 7,500 nautical miles

Detection Equipment: Type 271 Radar, ASDIC, HF/DF

Complement: 180 officers and men

Armament: 6 x 4-inch anti-aircraft guns

        4 x 13mm anti-aircraft guns

        1 x Quad 4 pdr 'Pom-Pom'

        Hedgehog mortar

        Depth charges

Produced in considerable numbers, the Flower Class corvettes such as HMS *Alisma* provided valuable service escorting Atlantic convoys. As well as serving with the Canadian Navy, a number were also supplied to the USA. (Imperial War Museum Photograph A-8488)

River Class frigate

Between 1941 and 1944 a total of 151 River Class frigates were built at shipyards across Great Britain. As well as with the Royal Navy, they served with the Royal Australian Navy, the Royal Canadian Navy, the Royal Netherlands Navy, the Free French Navy and the South African Navy.

Length: 91.9m

Beam: 11.1m

Displacement: 2,216 tons

Powerplant: 2 x Parsons steam turbines

Max Speed: 19 knots

Endurance: 7,200 nautical miles

Detection equipment: Type 271 Radar, ASDIC, HF/DF

Complement: 140 officers and men

Armament: 2 x 4-in. guns

4 x 20mm guns

Hedgehog mortar

Depth charges

Loch Class frigate

A total of 28 Loch Class frigates were completed, using prefabricated sections which were transported to shipyards for assembly. The majority served with the Royal Navy, though a handful also served with the Canadian and South African navies where they saw service during the Battle of the Atlantic as well as in other theatres.

Length: 87.2m

Beam: 11.7m

Displacement: 1,435 tons

Powerplant: 2 x Parsons steam turbines

Max Speed: 20 knots

Endurance: 9,500 nautical miles

Detection Equipment: Type 277 Radar, ASDIC, HF/DF

Complement: 114 officers and men

Armament: 1 x 4-in. gun

1 x Quad 4 pdr gun

2 x twin Oerlikon 20mm guns

8 x single Oerlikon 20mm guns

2 x Squid triple barrel mortars

Depth charges

US NAVY

Fletcher Class destroyer (DD)

This range of flush-deck destroyers was extremely popular with their crews. Rugged and capable of taking heavy punishment on the high seas and in combat, they were made in virtually every major shipyard in the USA. Over 170 were built, many of which were sold to former enemy countries, including Germany and Japan, after the war.

    Length: 114.7m
    Beam: 12m
    Displacement: 2,500 tons
    Powerplant: 2 x GE steam turbines
    Max speed: 36.5 knots
    Endurance: 5,500 nautical miles
    Detection equipment: SG Radar, HF/DF, ASDIC
    Complement: 329 officers and men
    Armament: 5 x 5-in. guns
              10 x 40mm guns
              10 x 20mm guns
              2 x depth charge racks
              6 x depth charge throwers

Evarts Class Destroyer Escort (DE)

The Evarts Class ships were built at the US Navy Yards at Boston, Mare Island, Philadelphia and Puget Sound. Although the initial order of 50 ships were made to fulfil British orders, the majority were requisitioned for service in the USN. None of this class were lost during combat. A final total of 72 of this class were completed.

    Length: 88m
    Beam: 10.7m
    Displacement: 1,140 tons
    Powerplant: 4 x V12 diesel engines
    Max speed: 21.5 knots
    Endurance: 5,000 nautical miles
    Detection equipment: SL Type Radar, ASDIC, HF/DF
    Complement: 198 officers and men
    Armament: 3 x 3-in. guns
              8 x 20mm guns
              1 x Quad 1-in.gun
              Hedgehog mortar
              Depth charges

The 1,500-ton USS *Benham*, lead ship of the Benham Class of destroyers. This vessel served on escort duties in the Atlantic in 1940, before the US entry into the war. (Naval Historical Collection)

Buckley Class Destroyer Escorts (DE)

The highly successful Buckley Class vessels were built at Bethlehem-Hingham, Quincy and San Francisco, Consolidated, Defoe and Dravo-Pittsburgh civilian yards, and the Charleston and Norfolk navy yards. The ships were prefabricated at various construction plants throughout the USA and welded together at the relevant shipyards. A total of 102 ships were built.

Length: 93.3m

Beam: 11.3m

Displacement: 1,740 tons

Powerplant: 2 x General Electric 4600kW steam turbines

Max speed: 23.6 knots

Endurance: 5,500 nautical miles

Detection equipment: Type SL Radar, ASDIC, HF/DF

Complement: 213 officers and men

Armament: 3 x 3-in. guns

9 x 20mm guns

1 x twin 40mm gun

Hedgehog mortar

Depth charges

Cannon Class Destroyer Escort (DE)

The Cannon Class DEs were built at the Navy Yard at Port Newark, and civilian yards at Dravo-Wilmington, Tampa and Western Pipe. A total of 72 were completed.

Length: 93.3m

Beam: 11.3m

Displacement: 1,600 tons

Powerplant: 4 x V12 diesel engines

Max Speed: 21 knots

Endurance: 10,800 nautical miles

Detection Equipment: SL Type Radar, ASDIC, HF/DF

Complement: 216 officers and men

Armament: 3 x 3-in. guns

8 x 20mm guns

2 x 40mm guns

Hedgehog mortar

Depth charges

Edsall Class Destroyer Escort (DE)

The Edsall Class were built at the Consolidated and Houston yards, a total of 85 being completed. Under the terms of the Lend-Lease agreement between the American and British government, the Royal Navy provided a number of Flower Class corvettes to the USA while the USN in turn provided several DEs, including the Edsall Class variety.

Length: 93m

Beam: 11.3m

Displacement: 1,590 tons
Powerplant: Fairbanks Morse diesel engines
Max speed: 21 knots
Endurance: 10,800 nautical miles
Detection equipment: SL Type Radar, ASDIC, HF/DF
Complement: 216 officers and men
Armament: 3 x 3-in. guns
          8 x 20mm guns
          2 x 40mm guns
          Hedgehog Mortar
          Depth charges

ENIGMA

A major factor in the success of the Allies from the second half of 1941 onwards was the cracking of the Enigma machine. Enigma was the name of a family of ciphering machines that used a complicated system of substitution alphabets and rotor machines which made German military transcripts almost impossible to crack by Allied intelligence. Polish Military Intelligence made the first significant breakthroughs in the 1930s but the constantly evolving system meant that it was a continuous battle to unravel this complex system. This was particularly true of the German Navy's Enigma ciphers which had always used more secure procedures. Thus it was crucial that cipher material be captured at sea to assist in the code-breaking. The first capture of Enigma material occurred in February 1940, when rotors VI and VII, the wiring of which was at that time unknown, were captured from the crew of U-33. On 9 May 1941, the Royal Navy captured U-110 with a complete Enigma machine, codebook, operating manual and other crucial information. Naval Enigma machines or setting books were captured from a total of seven U-boats and eight German surface ships during the war. One such captured U-boat was U-505, a Type IXC U-boat captured by the USN in 1944. The U-boat was towed back to America and the crew rescued. However, to protect the secret of the capture of the vital Enigma materials the prisoners were isolated from other POWs, the Red Cross was denied

Second Funkmaat Willi Anderheyden of U-564 on duty in the radio room and at work on the four-rotor Enigma machine introduced in 1942. Note his casual style of dress. [Royal Naval Submarine Museum]

access to them, and their families were informed that they had all been killed. The Enigma materials were eventually forwarded to Bletchley Park, the secret site of British codebreaking operations where they helped to continue cracking German naval codes and assisted in the eventual Allied victory in the Battle of the Atlantic. Today the U-505 is on display at the Museum of Science and Industry in Chicago.

By the beginning of 1945 the escorts had clearly won the Battle of the Atlantic. The speed with which the Allies were developing anti-submarine weaponry was fast outstripping the rate at which the Germans were developing counter-measures. Some of the German ideas, such as Alberich, a sonar-absorbing rubber coating, was a promising concept but lack of a suitable, effective adhesive prevented its widespread use.

The new Type XXI and Type XXIII boats with their streamline designs and very fast underwater speeds would have the ability to dodge many escort attacks or indeed, outrun some of the older escorts but ultimately reached the frontline in too few numbers to make a difference.

Postwar submarine design, greatly influenced by German developments, would once again bring the submarine back to the point where it could face its surface enemies on equal terms, but by the later stages of the war it was the Frigate/DE which had proven itself the more effective weapon.

The submarine had to destroy enemy merchant shipping, defend itself against escorts and when on the surface, potentially against aircraft. The Frigate/DE, unlike earlier escorts that were often obliged to fill more than one role, had only one purpose and one to which it owed its very existence, to kill submarines. It was this specialisation in its role which helped make the Frigate/DE more effective than any other escort type.

SUBMARINE WEAPONRY

Torpedoes

The basic weapon of any submarine is of course the torpedo. The torpedo was a highly sophisticated piece of weaponry which also meant that it was one of the most expensive weapons of the time. The U-Bootwaffe used two principal types, either steam-powered or electric-powered. At the outbreak of war, the mainstay of the force was the G7 torpedo. This existed in two variants, the G7a (TI) which was steam driven, powered by a chemical reaction from the burning of alcohol in a small onboard reservoir. The main drawback with this type was that it left a visible stream of bubbles in its 'wake' therefore eliminating the element of surprise. It had a top speed of some 44 knots and was detonated by an impact pistol on physically striking the hull of the enemy ship. The G7a was 7.1m in length and 53cm in diameter. It carried a warhead with 280kg of explosive and was therefore capable of huge destructive power. The G7a was manufactured to a very high standard and was thus rather expensive to produce.

The G7e (TII) was an electrically driven development of its predecessor. Of similar dimensions, it was powered by two small electrical motors, giving it a speed of 30 knots and range of 5km. Unlike its predecessor, it left no tell-tale wake and was much cheaper to produce.

The Germans suffered significant reliability problems with their torpedoes in the early part of the war, so much so that sabotage was suspected and a major investigation launched. So many operations were undermined by these faulty torpedoes that Dönitz exasperated by the situation, wrote in his war diary: "I do not believe that ever in the history of warfare have we been sent against the enemy with such useless weapons."

The device that detonated the warhead was the pistol, which was either magnetic or impact-operated. Most torpedoes in fact had both types of pistol and it was down to the captain to select the correct combination before launching the weapon. The magnetic pistol was triggered by the enemy vessel's magnetic field and was designed to explode underneath the hull. Such an explosion would have a devastating effect, potentially breaking the hull in two and sinking the ship immediately. Contact pistols comprised of four whiskers mounted at the tip of the nose. They were designed to react to a glancing blow which detonated the warhead. However, the pistol was only armed after a minimum run of 250m to prevent damage to the U-boat itself.

Malfunctioning pistols which meant that the torpedoes did not detonate had robbed the U-boats of some significant successes, including the destruction of

A G7e torpedo is loaded into the interior of a Type VII U-boat. This was an awkward and time-consuming task at the best of times. The torpedo room in a U-boat setting off on a mission with a full load of 'eels' was extremely cramped, especially as every spare inch of space was also crammed full of provisions. (Author's collection)

aircraft carriers and battleships as well as merchants. Incompetence and lack of development testing was found to be to blame for the problems with the magnetic torpedoes, and a number of senior figures in the navy's Torpedo Directorate were court-martialled and imprisoned. Problems with impact pistols were eventually traced to faulty hydrostatic valves which controlled the depth at which the torpedoes ran. Some were found to be insufficiently airtight so that they became affected by pressure changes inside the hull of the submarines as they altered depth. With their settings askew, many ran too deep and passed harmlessly under their targets. By late 1942 many of the torpedo problems had been cured but the number of lost opportunities for success due to faulty torpedoes up until then was immense.

Additional developments in torpedo technology led to the production of new guidance systems. The most important of these are listed below.

FaT (Federapparat Torpedo)

This guidance system, used on the G7, allowed the torpedo to run in a straight line towards its target area, then change to an "S" shaped course to increase its chance of finding a target.

LuT (Lagenunabhänginger Torpedo)

Again, using the basic G7 torpedo, this guidance system used a similar concept but with the additional benefit that the initial launch could take place at almost any suitable angle to the target.

Zaukönig (T5)

This was the principal acoustic torpedo type, with acoustic detectors in the nose which homed in on the cavitation noises caused by the propellers of the enemy ship. Its effectiveness was limited by its propensity to detonate when it hit the disturbed waters of a ship's wake and by the fact it was only able to detect cavitation from ships moving at between 10 and 18 knots. It was a development of the earlier Falke (T4) which saw only little use before being replaced by the Zaukönig.

Zaukönig II (T11)

This was a subsequent development that was tuned to the frequencies of ships' propellers rather than detecting cavitation, and was often used, fired from the stern tube of a U-boat, to defend against pursuing escorts.

Mines

Minelaying U-boats also scored a number of successes against Allied shipping using a range of mines.

Torpedo Mines (Torpedominen or TM)

These were cylindrical mines, the same diameter as the torpedo, which were ejected using the normal torpedo tubes of the submarine. Three types, TMA, TMB and TMC were used. TMA was 3.4m in length and carried a charge of 215kg of explosive. It was a moored mine, with a heavy baseplate and used in waters up to 270m in depth. TMB was shorter, at 2.3m but with a much bigger 580kg charge. It was laid on the seabed of shallower waters and was detonated by acoustic or magnetic signal. TMC was a larger version of TMB, 3.3m in length, carrying a 1,000kg charge.

Shaft Mines (Schachtminen or SM)

So called because they were carried in, and dropped from, vertical shafts in the submarine hull, these were 2.15m in length and carried a 350kg charge. They were used in water up to 250m in depth.

Mine Torpedo (Minentorpedo or MT)

As opposed to a torpedo-shaped mine like the TM, this weapon was an actual torpedo, but with a small mine fitted in place of the normal warhead. Fired in the standard fashion, it would reach the end of its run, sink to the seabed and then act as a normal magnetic/acoustic mine.

EMS mine (Einheitsmine Sehrohr Triebmine)

This small lightweight contact mine carrying only a 14kg charge was intended to be untethered and thus free-floating. To prevent its drifting from enemy into neutral or friendly waters, it was designed to activate almost immediately but to sink after 72 hours if undetonated.

Artillery

Two main types of artillery were carried by U-boats, these being the 88mm Schiffskanone C/35 and the 10.5cm Schiffskanone C/32. These were mounted on a pedestal fitting forward of the conning tower and could traverse through 360 degrees.

Both could fire either high explosive or armour-piercing shells and were crewed by three men: a gunner, loader and gun-layer. Additional crew members were used to keep the gun position supplied with ammunition.

U-BOAT WEAPONRY

1. Type T5 Zaukönig Acoustic torpedo designed to hone in on the cavitation noises caused by the propellers of the target ship.
2. Type G7e torpedo, which was driven by electric motors and therefore did not leave a tell-tale bubble trail.
3. Type G7a torpedo, the most expensive of the torpedoes.
4. Torpedomine which was fired through the torpedo tubes.
5. Schachtmine which were laid by minelaying U-boats.

Unless sea conditions were virtually flat and calm, a U-boat would not be a stable gun platform, so the gun tended to be used at fairly close range and only when the commander was fully confident that no enemy warships were near.

In action, the gun would be commanded by the second Watch Officer (IIWO) from his vantage point in the conning tower. Although in the early part of the war U-boats often did use the deck gun to sink smaller enemy merchantmen in order to save precious (and highly expensive) torpedoes, as the war progressed and anti-submarine measures improved in effectiveness, few U-boat commanders would risk surfacing and remaining in position long enough to sink a ship using gunfire (sometimes dozens or even hundred of hits were required to sink a larger vessel). By 1943, most Type VII U-boats had had their deck guns removed, which had the added benefit of reducing drag when underwater.

In addition to the larger calibre weapons, most U-boats also carried either 20mm or 37mm flak weapons which could also be used against surface targets. The 20mm flak weapons could be either single, twin (Zwilling) or quadruple (Vierling) barrelled. Although there are a number of examples of U-boats successfully fighting it out on the surface with enemy aircraft, and indeed for a time standing orders were that U-boats should do so rather than leave themselves virtually helpless against enemy aircraft during the dive, this was quickly changed and few boats were willing to risk combat with enemy aircraft.

ESCORT WEAPONRY

Depth Charge

The principal armament of the escort vessel in the war against the U-boat was the depth charge. At its simplest, this was a basic, cylindrical metal canister packed with between 150 and 300kg of explosive depending on the size of canister. A pressure-activated detonator was preset before launch to operate at a prescribed depth at which the submarine was thought to be submerged. Their shape caused them to tumble as they fell through the water and so subsequently a more aerodynamic teardrop-shaped container was introduced with a weighted 'nose' to ensure it dropped vertically through the water. Later in the war, magnetic impulse detonators were developed so that detonation was caused by the proximity of the submarine rather than by the charge simply reaching a predetermined depth.

It was rarely a case of a depth charge actually exploding against the structure of the submarine, though this would of course have had a catastrophic effect, but rather the immense pressure wave caused by the exploding depth charge in the vicinity of the submarine which would cause fatal damage. To achieve a 'kill', a depth charge would have to detonate within about 3m of the submarine, but an explosion within 10m could still cause severe damage.

Depth charges were usually either simply rolled off a ramp at the stern of the escort vessel, or alternatively thrown by a launcher device along the escort's side.

This relatively crude weapon had several drawbacks, not the least of which was that following the detonation of a charge, the degree of disturbance to the water meant that ASDIC could not be used for several minutes to try to relocate the enemy.

In addition, the depth charge would explode automatically at the preset depth so that the escort had no idea whether the explosion had actually caused any damage. Depth charges would normally take anything between 26 and 75 seconds to reach their predetermined depth for detonation, so that a U-boat whose sound detector operator heard the splash as the charges hit the water could potentially put on enough of a burst of speed to escape the 'kill zone' and perhaps only be shaken up rather than damaged or destroyed.

A special depth charge launcher known as 'Squid' was developed in 1944, which launched three depth charges at the same time, intended to land in a triangular pattern around the target. Even with a near miss, the combined effect of the three detonations could be sufficient to cripple or destroy a U-boat.

Hedgehog

This interesting but rather basic device, officially known as an Anti-Submarine Projector consisted of a spigot mortar located on the forward deck of the escort. A total of 24 small spigot rods projecting from a base-plate gave the apparatus its nickname. A mortar projectile with a tubular tail would then be placed on the spigot rods. Weighing around 30kg of which approximately half was the explosive charge (either TNT or Torpex), the projectile head measured 178mm in diameter.

The most basic form of depth charge, as shown here, was a steel drum filled with explosive with a pressure sensitive detonator preset to activate at a certain depth, and which was simply rolled off the stern of the escort vessel. (National Archives)

On firing, these projectiles would be launched forward of the ship to land in either a circular or elliptical pattern just over 200m ahead of the escort. These projectiles would explode on impact with the structure of any submarine. Unlike the case with the depth charge where an explosion could simply mean that the charge had detonated harmlessly at the predetermined depth, the detonation of a Hedgehog projectile by means of its contact fuse indicated that it had definitely hit its target and often only one or two hits were required to sink an enemy submarine, as opposed to many depth charges.

Early U-boats carried sound detector equipment known as *Gruppenhorchgerät* (GHG) installed in the hull side either side of the bow. Even though sound detection was only truly accurate when the boat was abeam of the object being detected, the degree to which sound carries in water meant that the splash of a heavy depth charge being dropped into the water could easily be heard. With the Hedgehog there was no such warning that they had been launched. Hedgehogs also had the advantage of not causing long-lasting disturbance to the water even when they had not hit their target as was the case with depth charges.

The one down-side of the Hedgehog mortar was that due to its smaller charge a direct hit was required and the cumulative damage caused by several close detonations which could be achieved with depth charges was not possible. Nevertheless the Hedgehog mortar achieved a success rate some three to four times that of the depth charge.

Artillery

The main armament types on escort vessels tended to be medium-calibre naval artillery pieces such as the 4-in. or 4.7-in. gun. Whilst these could be, and were often, used against submarines caught on the surface, they played a much smaller, less effective role in anti-submarine warfare than the depth charge or Hedgehog mortars. The 4-in. gun had a rate of fire of up to 15 rounds per minute, with a muzzle velocity of around 800m per second, firing a round of approximately 30kg to a range of around 18,000m (13,000m on older models).

The 4.7-in. gun had a rate of fire of around 10 rounds per minute, with a muzzle velocity of 800m per second, firing a 28kg round to a range of around 15,500m.

Though the main armament of the escort could be and was often used against U-boats caught on the surface, a small escort vessel being tossed around in an Atlantic swell was not a stable platform from which to aim such weapons. Add to this the small size of the target area being aimed at and one could see that use of the main artillery on board would never be the preferred method of tackling an enemy submarine.

In addition to the main armament, escorts carried varying degrees of small calibre anti-aircraft artillery which could also be used against surface targets, the leading types being the 37mm Bofors and 20mm Oerlikon cannon, the latter added to USN vessels from 1942 onwards.

Radar and its countermeasures

Whilst not weapons in the commonly accepted sense, that is they could not in themselves inflict damage, three of the most important pieces of technical equipment in the inventory of the escort vessel were Radar, ASDIC, and High Frequency

Direction Finding (HFDF or 'Huff Duff') equipment. Allied Radar was more advanced than its German equivalent, and by early 1941, ship-based, ten-centimetre wavelength Type 271 Radar with a range of up to 25 miles, was capable of detecting even the smallest wake caused by the periscope head of a U-boat as it cut through the waves. Within a year, well over two hundred escorts were fitted with this equipment and in November 1941, U-433 was sunk near Gibraltar after being detected by this equipment. The Germans did have limited success in their attempts to thwart detection by Allied Radar. The first efforts were in the development of a device, codenamed 'Metox', which in theory would detect the signals from Allied Radar at a

ESCORT WEAPONRY

1. 20mm Oerlikon cannon: Fired up to 450 rounds per minute and had a range of 2,000m.
2. Depth Charge thrower: This is the K-type variant which could throw up to 300kg of explosives. Area saturation with depth charges with a pre-set depth could cause severe damage even without a direct hit.
3. Hedgehog: Also known as an 'ahead throwing mortar', it could fire 24 projectiles at a time each carrying around 15kg of TNT. A direct hit was devastating, but a near miss would have absolutely no effect.

sufficient distance to allow the U-boat to dive to safety. Officially known as the FuMB 1 (Funkmesserbeobachter) this was introduced in July 1942. This equipment was used in conjunction with an extremely crude wooden cross-shaped antenna strung with wire and known as the 'Biscay Cross'. This antenna had to be rotated by hand. Unfortunately, it was soon discovered that the Metox's own emissions were detectable by Allied radar detection equipment, leading them straight to the U-boat. A subsequent improved version, the FuMB9 Zypern, was found also to be detectable by the British H2S radar detection system and it was not until the FuMB10 Borkum set that the U-boat had a radar detection system that was not itself detectable.

However, problems still remained, in that this equipment did not cover the full radar spectrum, a problem eventually solved in November 1943 by the FuMB7 Naxos. Naxos and Metox used together finally gave the U-boats excellent all-round radar detection capabilities. The range of capabilities of Naxos and Metox were finally combined in single systems with the introduction of the FuMB 24 Fliege and FuMB 25 Mücke systems in April 1944. So, eventually, albeit rather late in the war, the U-boats did have devices which would warn them that they were being detected by Allied Radar and that an attack was likely or imminent.

In terms of the U-boat itself detecting any enemy shipping, basic Radar equipment began to be installed on U-boats in 1940. The earliest operational type was the FuMo 29 (Funkmessortungs Gerät). This was predominantly used on the Type IX, but a few Type VII U-boats were also fitted with this equipment, easily visible on surviving

A depth charge explodes astern of HMS *Starling*. Mk VII depth charges, which were the standard anti-submarine weapon at the beginning of World War II, can be seen in the racks on the quarter-deck. The sea astern of this escort boils as the depth charge it has just dropped detonates. A direct hit was not required as the pressure wave created by the explosion was sufficient to cause significant damage even with a near miss. (IWM A22031)

The 20mm Oerlikon cannon with its crew. Such weapons would be used against U-boats forced to the surface to prevent their own gun-crews from manning their weapons. (National Archives)

photographs because of the twin horizontal rows of eight dipoles on the upper front part of the conning tower. The top row were transmitters and the lower row receivers. An improved version, FuMo30 was introduced in 1942 in which the tower mounted dipoles were replaced by a so-called retractable 'mattress' antenna which was housed in a slot in the tower wall. Bearing in mind that even on surface warships with tall superstructures, where the radar antennae would be placed at the top of the structure or high up on the mast to allow the radar the greatest possible range, it is easy to understand why a radar antenna mounted on the bridge of a vessel which sits as low in the water as does a submarine, might have limited range, and thus, limited effectiveness. This indeed was the case with the FuMo 29 and FuMo 30. Interference with the Radar signal by the ocean surface in heavy weather meant that enemy ships might be detected visually before being picked up on Radar.

The Allies also struggled with the use of Radar during the course of the war. Radar would not of course detect a fully submerged U-boat, and even if a boat had been detected on the surface or because of its protruding periscope, it may have fully submerged by the time the escort arrived on the spot. Instead, underwater detection was principally effected by a device known as ASDIC, (later to become more commonly referred to as SONAR) the name derived from the organization responsible for its development, the Anti-Submarine Detection Investigation Committee. ASDIC was housed in a metal dome beneath the ship's hull. At its most basic, it was simply a sound transmitter which send out a high-frequency 'ping' of sound underwater. If the ping was reflected back from a solid object, the time taken for the sound to reach the object and be reflected back would allow calculation of the distance of the object. The transmitter itself was fitted in a rotating mount so that both the direction (bearing) and distance could be established. The reality as one might expect, was far more complex. A number of factors would affect the quality of the signal. Different temperature layers in the water could reflect ASDIC signals so that enemy submarines could 'hide' under these layers, a tactic still used by submarines today to avoid detection. Heavy seas causing the escort to roll and pitch would create distortion, and noise interference caused by high speeds of the escort vessel itself could make successful detection difficult. In addition, ASDIC could return a false signal from things such as shoals of fish, and even the wakes of other vessels. It took a highly trained ear of an ASDIC operator to be able to filter out other false returns and home in on a genuine contact. On confirming a contact, the escort would rush to the spot at high speed, attempting to predict any last minute changes of depth or direction by the enemy. ASDIC contact would be lost as the submarine passed under the limited range of the ASDIC beam, usually around 300m. Thus a last minute change of course by the submarine could result in depth charges being dropped ineffectively, on its last known position as contact was lost.

The Germans attempted to defeat ASDIC detection by coating the hull of the submarine with a rubber substance known as *Alberich*. Considerable problems were encountered however in producing an effective adhesive. Tests showed that pieces of *Alberich* coating would come loose, causing drag and turbulence as the boat moved through the water and ironically, making it easier rather than more difficult, to detect. Eventually however, a successful adhesive was produced and subsequent testing showed the system to be very effective. Fortunately for the Allies, very few boats were treated with *Alberich* before the war ended.

20mm Oerlikon gunners of HMS *Starling* on arrival at Liverpool. Left to right: Able Seaman Edward O'Malley of Stockport, Cheshire (about to fix a fresh magazine of ammunition to the gun); Able Seaman John Smith, Able Seaman Edward Webster and Petty Officer William G Barnshaw. HMS *Starling* was part of 2nd Escort Group commanded by Captain F J Walker. The group was welcomed back to Liverpool by the First Lord of the Admiralty Mr A V Alexander after a record breaking North Atlantic patrol on which the group scored six U-boat kills.

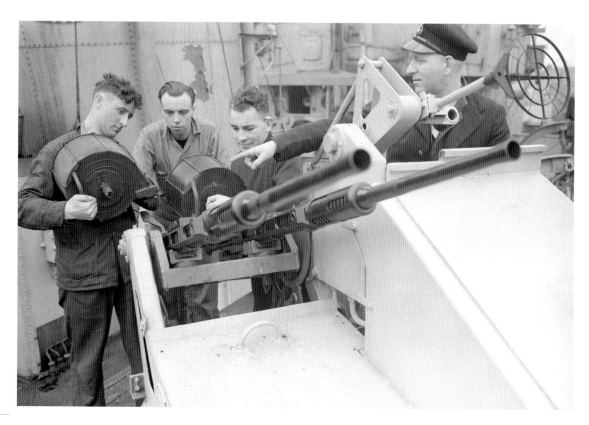

U-boats could also utilize a device known as 'Bold'. This was a simple device consisting of a metal canister packed with calcium-hydride, with an inlet valve to admit water. When launched, sea water would enter the canister and react with the calcium-hydride, releasing a dense volume of air bubbles. The canister was designed to hover at around 30m deep. The resultant disturbance in the water would give a sonar 'signature' very similar to the U-boat itself. Its purpose was to attract the attention of the escorts whilst the U-boat itself quietly slipped away un-noticed.

HFDFs were valuable tools for the detection of enemy submarines by Allied escort vessels. The idea of using two or more radio receivers to find the bearings of a radio transmitter and with the use of simple triangulation find the approximate position of the transmitter had been known about for years. Many shore-based installations were constructed around the North Atlantic and whenever a U-boat transmitted a message, HFDF could get bearings on the approximate position of the U-boat. This equipment did not require the ability to read or decode enemy signals, merely to detect their presence. At various points in its patrol, a U-boat would be required to surface and send radio messages back to B.d.U (i.e. to report having sighted a convoy). If a number of escort ships guarding a convoy were fitted with HFDF, the bearing from their individual locations to the source of the signal would allow its position to be accurately triangulated. HFDF equipment had the advantage of a much greater range than Radar, and could allow detection of a submarine whilst it was still some distance from a convoy allowing escort forces to race to the scene and tackle the threat before it reached striking distance of the merchant ships. Ultimately many of the more cautious U-boat commanders would avoid using their radios wherever possible, though this was primarily due to the fact that, unaware that the Allies had cracked the Enigma codes, they assumed that the number of U-boats being intercepted was because of radio transmissions being tracked.

THE COMBATANTS

U-BOAT CREWS

Surely every submariner has sensed in his heart the glow of the open sea, and the task entrusted to him, and felt as rich as a King and would have traded places with no one.
Grossadmiral Karl Dönitz

The rebirth of the U-Bootwaffe had begun in 1933 with the formation of the Unterseebootsabwehrschule or Anti-submarine Warfare School, whose purpose was the exact opposite of what the title suggests, and was used surreptitiously to train future submarine crews. At that time Germany was still prohibited from possessing submarines. In March 1935 Hitler repudiated the terms of the Treaty of Versailles and open U-boat construction began in earnest under former World War I U-boat commander Kapitän zur See Karl Dönitz.

U-boats were grouped into flotillas (Unterseebootflotillen) initially named after naval heroes of World War I before simple numbering replaced commemorative titles. The first U-boat flotilla, Unterseebootsflotille Weddigen, was named after Otto Weddigen, a U-boat Ace of the Imperial Navy, and commander of U-9.

As commander of U-boat forces, Dönitz held the title Führer der Unterseeboote (F.d.U.) or Leader of Submarines. As the force grew, the senior officers in command of submarines within an operational area would be given the title *Führer*, such as Führer der Unterseeboote West, and so on, whilst Dönitz and his successors in overall command would hold the title Befehlshaber der Unterseeboote, (B.d.U) or Commander of Submarines.

U-boat commands were established for operations from Norway (F.d.U Norwegen), from France (F.d.U West), in the Mediterranean (F.d.U Mittelmeer) and the Baltic (F.d.U Ost). Bases were even set up in Malaya in co-operation with the Imperial Japanese Navy for the so-called *Monsun* (Monsoon) boats which operated into the Indian Ocean and Pacific.

In the inter-war years, a significant number of books lauding the exploits of the U-boat men of World War I had been published and from its earliest days, the new U-Bootwaffe was seen very much as an elite force. Study of the demographics of U-boat personnel shows that it was not merely from traditional naval recruiting areas such as the coastal regions and sea ports that manpower was drawn, but from all across Germany.

With only a very limited amount of space to carry its small crew, successful operation of a U-boat required that each man in the crew be proficient not only in his own designated role, but also in at least one other, if not several, so that illness or injury of specific crewmen would not prevent the boat operating efficiently.

The petty officers' accommodation at mealtimes. Eight men also slept in this confined space. (Royal Naval Submarine Museum)

That being the case it is not surprising that when selecting crews for service in U-boats, the Kriegsmarine was particularly keen to recruit those with desirable skills, such as mechanics, fitters or electricians. Not too many of those who were unskilled labourers in peacetime would find their way into this new elite.

It is also perhaps not surprising that given the physical circumstances in which they would serve, U-boat men would be of small to medium stature. The two-metre high powerfully built giant who might look impressive on parade with an elite Guard Regiment would find life exceedingly difficult in the confines of a submarine whose hatches, bulkheads and cramped interior the crew needed to be able to navigate quickly in emergency circumstances.

Those recruited into the U-boat service were also expected to be in robust good health and have no dental problems (treating toothache in an operational U-boat in the middle of a long war cruise would be difficult, unpleasant and most likely extremely painful), to have a clean police record and not to be a member of any political party. Needless to say there would have been many within the U-boat arm who *were* avid supporters of the regime, but the Navy as a whole was not overtly political and Dönitz, well aware of the need for each U-boat man to be able to trust the fellow crewmates on whom his life may well depend, avoided allocating the despised National Socialist Leadership Officers (broadly equivalent to the Soviet Union's 'Political Commissars') to U-boat service.

Only already fully trained sailors were accepted for service on submarines. Once allocated to U-boats they underwent further rigorous training, both theoretical and practical. All U-boat men needed to know and understand exactly how a submarine was

Recruiting posters for the Kriegsmarine. Note that the image of the submarine features prominently in the design of the poster on the left, indicative of the high esteem in which the U-boats were held by the German public.

designed and constructed, how it operated including the diesel and electric propulsion systems, and be able to operate a range of specialist machinery, including the weapons systems. Simulated escapes from sunken submarines also had to be practised.

Crews were often allocated to a new boat whilst it was still under construction, and used this opportunity to familiarize themselves with every inch of their new vessel. This time was known as *Baubelehrung* (literally Builder Instruction). Once commissioned the boat and its crew would undergo extensive practise exercises in the relative safety of the Baltic Sea before being judged fit for combat service or *Frontreif*. All of this specialized U-boat training could typically take around 11 months. However, this would change under the pressures of wartime, and the growing need for replacement of wartime losses saw the gradual reduction of this period down to as little as two or three months.

Officers required even more extensive training, usually obtained by serving as a Watch Officer on an operational boat under an experienced commander before undergoing intensive U-boat commander training and taking command of their own boat.

Given that service on U-boats was one of the most dangerous of all branches of the armed services and life expectancy, especially in the second half of the war, being low with around three quarters of the force being lost in action, U-boat men were allowed a much greater degree of freedom than other servicemen. When on operations, men were generally allowed to wear whatever they felt most comfortable with and discipline, in general, was fairly relaxed. This is not of course to suggest that these men were indisciplined, but rather that what was expected was self-discipline rather than discipline rigidly imposed by the boat's officers.

KAPITÄNLEUTNANT KLAUS HEINRICH BARGSTEN

A U-boat commander noted for his willingness to tackle escorts as well as merchants, Klaus Bargsten was born in Bad Oldesloe on 31 October 1911. He joined the navy as an officer aspirant on 3 April 1936. He attended the Ships Artillery School in Kiel and the Naval Academy at Mürwick. He joined the tender *Nordsee* for navigation training in October 1936 continuing this training aboard the cruiser *Leipzig* . Throughout 1937 he continued intensive training including courses at Coastal Artillery School and Naval Signals School before, in October, joining the State Yacht *Aviso Grille* for sea training as a Midshipman.

Bargsten was commissioned as Leutnant zur See in April 1938. Having applied for transfer to submarines, Bargsten was sent to the U-boat training school at Neustadt in April 1939 and was still undergoing the traditional intensive training for this role when war broke out in September of that year. He was appointed as a watch officer aboard U-6 in the training flotilla and in October 1939 promoted to Oberleutnant zur See.

Bargsten's combat career began in June 1940 when he joined U-99 under top ace Otto Kretschmer and carried out several combat patrols as Watch Officer, sufficiently impressing Kretschmer that the latter recommended him for U-Boat commander training.

Following additional training, Bargsten took command of U-563 and took her on her first war patrol on 31 July 1941. This patrol was uneventful but the second patrol was to be dramatically different. Setting off from his base in Brest, Bargsten took his boat in search of Convoy OG 75. Just as he made contact with the enemy, the U-boat was attacked by enemy aircarft and forced tu dive. Patrolling west of Gibraltar, Bargsten then lay in wait for Convoy HG 75. Contact was made just after midnight on 23 October, when Bargsten spotted an escorting destroyer. This was in fact HMS *Cossack,* a Tribal Class destroyer, which had gained fame when it intercepted the German auxiliary *Altmark* and was carrying several hundred British seamen from the Merchant Navy who had been captured by the pocket battleship *Admiral Graf Spee* . The German ship was in Norwegian waters at that time and with Norway still neutral the boarding of the German ship by the British was technically an illegal act. That, combined with the

killing of several of *Altmark's* crew members, had enraged the Germans. Bargsten launched a torpedo at the *Cossack* which hit just forward of the bridge, blowing off the forward part of the ship, killlling over 150 officers and men. Bargsten continued his attack on HG 75 until his torpedoes were expended and then returned to Brest.

In June 1942, Bargsten was given command of a new boat, U-521, a Type IX and was promoted to Kapitänleutnant zur See on 1 August.

Shortly after his return from another successful cruise, on 16 March 1943, he was awarded the Knight's Cross.

Bargsten's next and final patrol was off the US coast. He was shadowing a convoy when one of its escorts, a small patrol craft PC 565, detected the submarine and dropped depth charges causing severe damage. Critically damaged and forced to the surface, U-521 came under heavy gunfire from PC 565 and Bargsten, first onto the conning tower, ordered his crew to abandon ship. However, the submarine went under before the crew could evacuate, and Bargsten was the only one saved, spending the remainder of the war in a POW Camp in Florida.

The radio shack on an operational U-boat. As well as manning the radio, the crewman on duty at this station was also the boat's 'DJ' and would play popular music to help the crew relax during the long periods of inaction which often occurred for the off-watch personnel whilst the U-boats hunted for targets. (Francois Saez)

In general, although exceptions occurred, this was successful, with most crews developing a tremendous team spirit, appreciating the more relaxed atmosphere, but able and willing to obey orders instantly and without question when in action.

When home on leave, U-boat men were often allowed far more tolerance when 'letting off steam' as they relaxed after an arduous war cruise, such tolerance being a small price to pay for the sacrifices they were prepared to make on the battlefield – senior commanders were known to 'pull strings' for their men if they had fallen foul of the authorities when on leave.

As a former U-boat man himself, Dönitz expected loyalty, bravery and, if necessary, self-sacrifice from his men. In return he made every effort to ensure their welfare was provided for. Whenever possible, Dönitz would personally greet returning boats to congratulate them on their successes and chat with commanders and crews. He would ensure that men were given adequate leave, and even made his own personal train available to transport men from their ports back to Germany to ensure as little leave time as possible was wasted in transit. Ski-resorts and other facilities were made available for his men to relax on leave and the best of rations were provided.

However, U-boat commanders as well as their men were known to test the patience of the authorities by their disrespectful attitude towards the regime. In one well-reported incident, as U-564 was guided into port by its commander, Kapitänleutnant Sühren and as the boat approached the quayside where various dignitaries were ready to celebrate his safe return, Sühren called out, 'Are the Nazis still in power?' When the reply 'Yes' came back, Sühren ordered 'Full Astern'.

The interior of an operational U-boat was not a pleasant environment. Restricted amounts of fresh water meant little was available for luxuries such as washing or shaving and liberal amounts of cologne were used to cover the smell of unwashed bodies. An average of 50 men shared the tiny interior served by one equally tiny toilet, (two were provided but one usually given over to storage space). Condensation in the hot interior meant that fresh food spoiled rapidly and the interior was soon permeated by the foul smell of oil, diesel fumes, rotting food, and the sweat and bodily smells of the crew. Only towards the end of a war cruise when supplies and torpedoes had been exhausted did the available space inside the boat become anywhere near tolerable.

It takes a special breed of sailor to be prepared to serve in the most unpleasant conditions and in the knowledge that their chances of survival were extremely low. There were undoubtedly, as previously mentioned, individuals within the U-Bootwaffe who were fiercely loyal to the Nazi regime, but as with most small bands of elite servicemen, their immediate loyalties lay with their crew comrades, their commander and to the U-Bootwaffe. Even today, the majority of survivors of the U-boat service are fiercely loyal to the memory of their comrades and their commander, Karl Dönitz.

ALLIED CREWS

Overall command of the Royal Navy was vested in the Board of the Admiralty, with the First Sea Lord as Chief of Naval Staff assisted by five Sea Lords. They exerted command over a Navy divided into fleets, four in all by the end of the war – the Home Fleet, Mediterranean Fleet, Pacific Fleet and East Indies Fleet. The Home Fleet was the fleet operational in the Atlantic and specific responsibility for escorting the Atlantic convoys fell to the Western Approaches Command within this fleet.

Those who served fell into four broad categories:

Active Service personnel: the "regulars";

RNR (Royal Naval Reserve): former active service ;

RNVR (Royal Naval Volunteer Reserve): broadly equivalent to the Territorial Army, but after the outbreak of war for officers only;

Hostilities Only: created after the outbreak of war for non-officer ranks.

Due to the manpower needs of the navy in wartime, far more officers were needed than Active Service personnel could provide and a huge proportion, estimated as high as 88 percent, of the navy's officers during World War II were RNVR.

All of the navy's major surface warships were commanded by regular Active Service officers which means that the vast majority of the smaller escort vessels engaged in the war against the U-boats were of the RNVR. Generally speaking larger escorts such as destroyer-sized vessels would be commanded by either a commander or lieutenant-commander and smaller vessels by a lieutenant.

The lower ranks whether signed on for active service for a minimum of 12 years, or those conscripted 'for the duration', would be allocated to ships as required on completion of their training, with no choice as to whether they served on a huge battleship or aircraft carrier, or a tiny corvette. Sailors joining a ship's company would normally remain with that ship until it was decommissioned. Indeed in some cases a sailor might find himself moved from one of the biggest warships in the navy to one of the smallest. As an example, when the battleship *Royal Sovereign* was decommissioned from the Royal Navy and given to the Soviets to aid in their war effort, many of the battleship's former crewmen were transferred to Destroyers escorting the Russian Convoys and would be required to learn how to operate a new vessel and new tactics.

Unlike service on U-boats which was entirely different to working on normal ships, and required intensive specialized training, those allocated to anti-submarine vessels would have undergone perfectly normal training and only required a small amount of specialist training to use ASW equipment and weaponry. On being transferred to anti-submarine forces, Royal Navy crews would undergo intensive training, predominantly at HMS *Nimrod* at Campbelltown, working from early morning to late at night as they learned to use various detection equipment such as ASDIC and the various ASW weaponry such as Hedgehog, depth charges etc. This training could often include practical experience tracking and making dummy attacks on 'friendly' British submarines.

In the US Navy, the majority of officers and men serving on DEs were from the reserves. Most such vessels were commanded by reservist officers ranked at senior

Two posters distributed during the Battle of the Atlantic by the Office for War Information in the United States. (NARA)

grade lieutenant or lieutenant commander, and generally with previous experience on subchasers or minesweepers.

In many ways, the crews of the Allied escort vessels were similar to the U-boat crews they hunted. In both cases, the crew numbers were modest in size. Even the larger escorts, the destroyers, had a crew of approximately 130. In both cases the commander was often a fairly junior officer. Destroyers and other escorts were often commanded by those who had not chosen a specialist career such as gunnery or torpedoes and duty in the escort services was often a route by which a relatively junior officer could receive his own command faster than in other branches of the navy.

On most escorts, the average age of the juniors ranks was under 20 and the senior ranks, including officers and commanding officers, under 30. The junior ranks on these small warships were often without previous combat experience and so the presence of a cadre of good-quality experienced senior ranks was essential.

As with the Royal Navy, US DE crews would have undergone regular naval training that would then be enhanced by training on ASW operations. It was often the case that a newly commissioned DE crew member or even one with combat experience, would be rotated through one of the training establishments to provide new crews with 'on the job' training on exactly the type of vessel in which they would ultimately serve. In some cases this involved training the cadre crew for another DE still under construction. Much of the training of US DE crews took place at the naval base at Norfolk, Virginia. The *Haines*, *Silverstein* and *Brennan* are only three examples of the many DEs that took part in the training programme. All officers intended for ASW duty would undergo intensive training at the Sub Chaser Training Centre at Miami, which was set up in March 1942.

CAPTAIN DONALD MACINTYRE DSO, DSC RN

Born in 1904, Donald Macintyre joined the Royal Navy in 1920 and served as a Midshipman on the light cruiser HMS *Despatch*. After attending the Royal Naval College in Greenwich he was promoted to sub-lieutenant in February 1925 and joined the Destroyer HMS *Vanquisher* in the Mediterranean. Serving with this ship he was promoted to lieutenant in November 1926.

A change in direction came for Macintyre in 1927 when he joined the Fleet Air Arm and flew from the aircraft carriers HMS *Hermes* in the Far East and HMS *Courageous* in home waters.

A brief return to sea duty in September 1933 was followed in January 1934 by a return to flying which lasted until November of that year when he was promoted to lieutenant-commander and returned to sea duty.

In February 1935, Macintyre took command of the sloop HMS *Kingfisher*, where he gained experience in anti-submarine tactics. He remained with her for one year before taking command first of the Minesweeper HMS *Widness* in the Mediterranean, then of HMS *Defender* in the Far East.

As war clouds gathered over Europe, Macintyre returned to home waters where he was briefly given command of the old V Class destroyer HMS *Venomous* and the H Class HMS *Hesperus*. On 31 December 1940 Macintyre was promoted to commander and in March 1941 took command of HMS *Walker*. With this ship, an elderly destroyer, well past her best, came command of the newly-formed 5 Escort Groups which also included four more destroyers and two Flower Class corvettes. It was with this escort group that Macintyre was responsible for the destruction of U-99 and U-100.

On 6 May 1941, Macintyre's successes brought him the Distinguished Service Order (DSO).

In June 1942 Macintyre was appointed to command Escort Group B2, consisting of two destroyers and six flower class corvettes, flying his own flag in the destroyer HMS *Hesperus*. In December 1942 Macintyre sank U-357 by ramming during a night attack on Convoy HX 219. Macintyre's greatest successes came in 1943 when, his ship, now armed with the deadly Hedgehog mortars, sank U-191, U-186 and badly damaged U-223.

On 9 March 1943, Macintyre was awarded the Bar to his DSO for his further successes against the U-boats and on 7 September this was followed by a second Bar.

In March 1944 Macintyre took over HMS *Bickerton*, one of the US-built Buckley class Destroyer Escorts, classed as frigates in the Royal Navy, in his new role as commander of 5 Escort Group.

With this new command, Macintyre sank U-765 and U-269. The former success would bring him the Distinguished Service Cross (DSC) in September of that year.

In August 1944, whilst sailing in escort of the carrier HMS *Nabob*, both Macintyre's frigate and the carrier were hit by torpedoes from U-354.

Macintyre's ship was severely damaged and a large number of her crew killed. The survivors were taken off and the wreck sunk by torpedoes from one of the other escorts.

Captain Macintyre served ashore for the remainder of the war, as commander of the RN Air Station at Machrihanish, his commands having sunk a total of seven U-Boats including those of two of Germany's greatest aces, Otto Kretschmer and Joachim Schepke.

After the war, Macintyre was promoted to full captain and served for a time as Naval ADC to King George VI.

After retiring from the navy, Macintyre became a respected naval historian and highly successful author.

Serving in small flotillas and operating in tandem with other vessels identical in size gave rise to a close kinship between Allied escort crews. Also, as with service on the U-boats, life on an escort could be extremely uncomfortable and unpleasant in certain weather conditions.

DEs were often referred to as 'Baby Destroyers'. Like their larger fleet destroyer counterparts, they were long narrow vessels, built for agility and speed but in rough weather they, or rather their crews, suffered as their ships rolled and plunged, bucked, twisted and shuddered in heavy seas. Seasickness was endemic. Simply existing on a small warship being tossed around in the North Atlantic was hazardous, even without the enemy to contend with. Anything not lashed down was likely to be thrown around and become a missile that could injure crewmen. It has been suggested that the living space available per crewman on a DE was one-sixth of that allocated to an inmate of the US prison system!

Whilst British sailors who served in the US-built escorts which were taken into the Royal Navy as Captain Class frigates found the accommodation generally of a higher standard than in British ships, they were certainly not luxurious vessels. Although the provision of ice-cream makers, iced-water drinking fountains and coffee percolators seemed the height of luxury to junior ranking British sailors, many crew members complained about the extremely primitive toilet facilities, something they shared with their opposite numbers in the U-Bootwaffe. On a typical British V & W Class destroyer, five open toilet 'stalls' with no doors to provide privacy, served around 150 men, as opposed to two enclosed WCs on a U-boat serving around 50.

Being at sea for weeks at a time – a common occurrence for both Allied and U-boat crews – also meant food deprivations as supplies began to run low. Here one Allied seaman describes how crews desperately tried to make their provisions last while their convoy travelled to Gourock in Scotland:

... our stores of food were diminishing rapidly and it was a matter of tightening our belts. The worst thing of all was our bread supply. First the crusts went green, which wasn't too bad because we could cut the crusts off. Then the inside of the bread started going green. This we covered with jam and pretended it wasn't even there. After a while, when the bread was really inedible, we had to go onto what is known in the services as hardtack. This is a form of biscuit, just like a dog's biscuit, and as long as your teeth were good you had no problem eating them – and if you had a cup of tea you always dunk them to soften them up. Besides running out of bread, our meat supply had also been diminished, so we had to go onto another good old standby – tins of corned beef... Fortunately we were on the homeward journey and were looking forward to getting back to Gourock and some real food.[1]

In stormy winter seas, crewmen would literally have to take their life in their hands to move from one end of the ship to the other. Lifelines had to be rigged for crewmen to hold on to as their vessel was tossed around by heavy seas and in extreme cases crews would often be confined to their duty stations as it was simply too dangerous

---

1   Petty Officer Engineer Mechanic George Fogden Escorting Convoys in the North Atlantic on HMS Bulldog, articled submitted as part of BBC World War 2 People's War Oral History Project

to move around. This was particularly true in operations in the North Atlantic during winter months, or on duty escorting convoys to the Soviet port of Murmansk.

When serving in cold northern waters, heat created by engines and machinery below decks resulted in huge amounts of condensation, meaning that clothing was always damp. Things were little better when serving in hot southern waters where the heat below decks would be almost unbearable.

On long-haul trips, escorts would often have to refuel at sea, a dangerous and difficult task at the best of times, but in the North Atlantic in winter, a real challenge to test the nerves of even the most experienced sailors, and the danger of encountering the enemy unexpectedly was ever-present. Petty Officer Engineer Mechanic George Fogden, who served on board HMS *Bulldog*, subsequently recounted one re-fuelling episode that went slightly awry:

> ...we were running desperately short of fuel... We were by then approaching the Azores and, being a neutral country, we could not enter the harbour without permission. Our captain radioed the British Consulate on the Azores and explained our situation... A response was immediately put into operation and we were allowed to enter harbour, where to our relief an oil tanker was at anchor. After careful manoeuvring and tying up on the starboard side of the tanker, the next operation was to connect up the fuel pipes... However, after we started taking on fuel we noticed that on the other side of the tanker also refuelling was a German U-boat... This caused great consternation because if the U-boat left harbour before us it could be waiting when we got out and we would be an obvious target for their torpedoes...[2]

In this instance, HMS *Bulldog* managed a lucky escape after rapidly refuelling and heading out to the relative safety of the high seas.

2   ibid.

Battle training for U-boat hunters – Royal Navy Training at Tobermory, Mull, Scotland 1944. As part of their training on board HMS *Western Isles* naval ratings prepare to launch the improvized raft they have built in seven minutes from rubber cylinders, old spares and other materials. In order to make this training as realistic as possible, rum and water jars and provisions are also attached to the raft, and the sailors must jump onto the raft in the same way as they would in an emergency situation. (IWM D20274)

COMBAT

One thought it was going to be bloody, but one had the feeling that we'd been pretty good on the sea for many, many years, and somehow we'd get through.
Rear-Admiral John Adams, Royal Navy

Almost as soon as war broke out, the convoy system was authorized once again. However, the problem was that there was a huge shortage of available escorts and, initially, escorts could only be provided for ships entering and leaving the waters around Great Britain and not all the way across the Atlantic.

Every available ship would have to be used to help supply Great Britain, even the elderly, slow vessels. Convoys were therefore classed as either 'fast' convoys or, for those with the older vessels, 'slow' convoys. The slow convoys would cross the Atlantic in somewhere around 20 days, the fast convoys some five days less. But even the "fast" convoys had an average speed of just 9 knots.

With a top speed of around 17 knots, any U-boat wouldn't have a problem in pursuing and catching a merchant which could attain only 9 knots. However, by travelling in convoy, merchants offered a degree of protection to each other. Many merchants were armed with one or two guns which could offer resistance to a U-boat on the surface. Not too many U-boats would wish to trade gunfire with any vessel that might risk damage to its pressure hull and prevent it diving. Merchants could also attempt to ram submarines. It was much safer therefore for a submarine to close with the convoy whilst submerged, but that in return would result in its maximum speed being reduced to around 8 knots, making it difficult to keep pace, especially if it also had to take evasive action to avoid escorts.

Regardless of these limitations, in the first month of the war alone, 41 ships totalling over 150,000 tons were sunk by U-boats. This despite the small number of

U-boats available to Dönitz. Indeed, one full year after the start of the war, in September 1940, there were still only 24 operational U-boats. This figure was two less than the submarine force with which Germany began the war due to the losses of U-39 and U-42, which had been sunk when they had engaged British warships.

The first major convoy battle of the war came in October 1940. Convoy SC 7 was a slow convoy from Nova Scotia heading to Liverpool and consisted of 35 merchants, many of which were smaller, elderly vessels with cargoes ranging from steel and iron ore to wooden pit-props destined for Britain's coal mines. However, one large Admiralty tanker was included, as was a freighter carrying military vehicles. The escort strength for this large convoy consisted of just one small sloop, HMS *Scarborough*. It was later reported that many ships' captains were unhappy at travelling in such a lightly guarded convoy and would have preferred to take the risk of travelling alone.

The convoy set sail on 4 October and enjoyed 12 uneventful days but as the convoy entered the Western Approaches, it was attacked by a group of seven U-boats whose commanders included the aces Herbert Schulze and Otto Kretschmer. This was the second co-ordinated Wolfpack attack of the war and on that first day, only a single small straggler, the SS *Trevisa* was sunk.

Men from all frigates of the 21st Escort Group of Captain Class frigates with their Jolly Roger on board HMS *Conn* after returning from a patrol in which they sank three U-boats and a possible fourth. Five U-boats is the group's total of kills. Crossed scalpels at the bottom indicate two surgical operations performed at sea during patrols. (IWM A28198)

The sound-detector operator on a U-boat practising timing the seconds between the splash of a depth charge as it hit the water and its detonation. These seconds were crucial as a skilled U-boat captain could use them to apply a burst of speed and manoeuvre away from the danger area. (Royal Naval Submarine Museum)

Despite the arrival of two more escorts, the sloop HMS *Fowey* and the corvette HMS *Bluebell* on the following day, the U-boats attacked again and sank three more ships including the tanker. On 18 October the sloop HMS *Leith* and corvette HMS *Heartsease* arrived to augment the escort force but the Germans responded by sinking eight more ships. The destruction peaked during the following day when, despite the best efforts of the escorts, the U-boats sank a further nine ships, bringing their total to 20 ships out of the original total of 35. In all, over 79,500 tons of ships had been sunk without the loss of a single submarine. Otto Kretschmer in U-99 had accounted for seven of the ships that had been sunk. The carnage in fact may well have continued but for the arrival of Convoy HX 79 and the rich picking there drew the U-boats away from SC 7.

But it didn't always go the way of the U-boat. On 25 February, Gunther Prien in U-47 began an attack on convoy OB 293. This convoy was provided with four escorts, two of which were fitted with Radar. The exact circumstances of U-47's loss are not known but Prien never returned from his attack on this convoy. So great was the impact that it was assumed his loss would have on the nation's morale, that Prien's loss was kept secret for some time afterwards, only being admitted to in May of that year.

On 17 March 1941, two more of Germany's top aces, Otto Kretschmer in U-99 and Joachim Schepke in U-100, were involved in an attack on convoy HX 112. This convoy had the luxury of what was for this point in the war, a fairly strong escort including two corvettes and five destroyers, one of which, HMS *Vanoc*, was equipped with Radar. At just after 0130 hours, U-100 was forced to the surface after suffering severe damage in a depth-charge attack by escorts. Once surfaced, the engine room crew were unable to start the U-boat's diesel motors. As U-100 attempted to limp away on her electric motors, she was rammed amidships by HMS *Vanoc*. Schepke, still on the conning tower, was crushed against the periscope pedestal by the destroyer's bows' shearing off both his legs. Only six of the crew were rescued. Petty Officer Walter Edney gave this account of the moment in his memoirs compiled after the war.

... the silhouette of a U-boat could be seen on the surface, so without hesitation our Captain gave the order to 'Stand by to Ram'. This we did, in no uncertain manner, at full speed, hitting the U-boat amidship and toppling her over. It brought *Vanoc* to a sudden standstill, embedded in the U-boat which was only cleared by both engines, full astern. The U-boat rose high in the air and sunk, the Captain still on the bridge wearing his white cap but badly injured went down with her... We next swept the surface of the waters with our searchlight in order to pick up survivors. I well remember and will do always, the cries of those men in the icy waters 'Camerade'. In my youth my bitterness towards them was extreme. They had sunk our ships and many of our seamen drowned at sea... I just had to shout 'leave them there'. Fortunately perhaps the older members of our crew had more compassion and pulled up the side as many as they could, before the next alarm.[3]

Meanwhile Otto Kretschmer in U-99 had managed to sneak into the centre of the convoy on the surface under cover of darkness and, firing off a salvo of torpedoes from both bow and stern tubes, sank five ships totalling 34,000 tons in quick succession. As the escorts concentrated their efforts on U-100, Kretschmer brought his boat out ahead of the enemy ships but as he circled the convoy to bring himself on a heading for home, the watch officer on the bridge spotted a destroyer and instinctively sounded the alarm. Kretschmer may have had a chance of remaining undetected on the surface, as the destroyer which had been spotted, HMS *Walker*, was not fitted with Radar. However, U-boat crews were trained to react instantly to an alarm call and the boat immediately dived, at which point it was quickly located by HMS *Walker*'s ASDIC and subjected to a furious barrage of depth charges. The U-boat plunged out of control to a depth of over 200 metres before it could be halted. Blowing compressed air into the ballast tanks halted its plunge but had the effect of shooting it back up onto the surface where it came under HMS *Walker*'s guns. With his deck gun destroyed and his boat mortally wounded, Kretschmer had no hope of escape. He signalled the enemy warships that he was abandoning ship and asked for his crew to be saved. Fortunately for him, the British took the risk of stopping to pick up survivors and all but three crew members of U-99 were saved, including Kretschmer himself. In just under 18 months of combat service, Kretschmer had established a score of enemy tonnage sunk of 274,000, which would never be surpassed even by those who went on to serve throughout the remainder of the war.

These three German U-boat aces had scored tremendous success in the opening months of the war but increasingly the implementation of an effective convoy system and thet technological developments of Radar and ASDIC were beginning to reap the rewards for the Allies. Moreover, the loss of these three aces was a great blow to morale in Germany, where they were popular heroes. In his memoirs Dönitz noted that, 'the death of

Navigators played a vital role within a U-boat as they plotted the interception of Allied convoys as well as U-boat rendezvous that occurred across the hundreds of miles of Atlantic Ocean. Here StabsObstrm Karl 'Stuckorl' Limburg, a veteran of World War I, plots a course for U-564. (Royal Naval Submarine Museum)

3   Extract from *Fortune without Fame*, a autobiography by Lt.Cdr Walter P. Edney written for his family and included on the BBC WW2 People's War online archive.

Prien and Schepke and the loss of U-99 were particularly heavy blows to me and my staff.' Josef Goebbels also commented in his war diary on 10 April 1941 on what had been a disastrous week for the U-boats, 'Kretschmer in English captivity. Prien and Schepke probably lost. Our three best U-boat commanders in one day. This is dreadful. We publish nothing about for the moment. The people will be sad.'

The U-Bootwaffe's bad luck continued when on 9 May 1941 another of the top aces, Helmut Lemp in U-110, was detected by ASDIC during an attack on convoy OB-318. Subjected to a devastating depth-charge attack by HMS *Aubrietia*, the U-boat was forced to the surface and its crew abandoned ship, under fire from the escorts.

By now, the effects of placing inexperienced and inadequately trained crews on U-boats in an effort to build the strength of the submarine fleet as fast as possible was having its effect. In September 1941, convoy SC 42 was en route from Sydney in Australia to Great Britain. Having safely navigated its way to the North Atlantic, it was finally intercepted by U-85 near the east coast of Greenland. The location of the convoy now known, more U-boats vectored in on its location three of which, U-81, U-82 and U-432 launched an attack under the cover of darkness and each sank one merchantman. U-652 scored hits on two more vessels but failed to sink them, one of the damaged vessels subsequently being despatched by U-372.

Next morning, U-85 torpedoed and sank another merchant but was herself detected and attacked by the escort USS *Roper* and sunk. The Germans were by no means having it all their own way, and U-501, on its way to join the attack, was forced to dive by an Allied flying boat, was depth charged and sunk by the escorts HMCS *Moosejaw* and HMCS *Chambly*. During the next night, the U-boats pressed home their attack with some success, with U-82, U-202, U-207 U-432 and U-433 sinking eight ships between them. This battle had brought about the destruction of 16 merchant ships, but the battle had not been one sided, with two U-boats also being lost.

HMS *Vanoc*, commanded by Lt Cdr Deneys, rammed and sank the U-100 on 17 March 1941. (Imperial War Museum Photograph A-4596)

Even more disastrous, an attack on convoy HG 76 at the end of 1941 saw five U-boats lost during one convoy attack including U-127, U-131, U-434, U-574 and U-567, the latter commanded by another 'ace of the deep', Engelbert Endrass. By this point in the war, some 1,124 ships had been sunk by U-boat action, totalling around 5.3 million tons, but the Allies would soon benefit by the increased production strength that the United States would bring to the table following her official declaration of war. In contrast, the German wartime economy would struggle to re-build her depleting U-boat fleet as well as adequately crew it.

U-boat commanders were not slow to realize that with ASDIC designed to detect boats underwater, operating on the surface at night under the cover of darkness would make them extremely difficult to detect. The escorting warships sat much higher in the water than the U-boat and if the latter was trimmed to sit low in the water, it would take extremely good luck for an escort's lookouts to spot her silhouette. Bolder commanders like Otto Kretschmer had begun making their attacks on the surface, often taking the U-boat right into the convoy, believing that no British naval escort would

think that any U-boat commander would be mad enough to take his boat right in amongst the merchants he was attacking. Ultimately of course the advent of ship-borne Radar would mean that a U-boat on the surface was every bit as vulnerable to detection as one underwater, if not more so.

However, grouped into wolfpacks, these U-boats sank vast numbers of merchant ships in the Atlantic. This peaked in 1942 with 1,662 merchant ships being sunk. Stronger escort forces were required to counter the wolfpack tactics, while a vessel designed specifically to attack the U-boat itself – the DE/frigate – was crucial.

Probably the most famous convoy battle of the war centered around Convoy PQ 17 heading from Iceland to Murmansk. PQ 17, consisting of 35 ships packed with military equipment for the Soviet Union, had set sail on 27 June with a heavy escort including three minesweepers, four armed trawlers, five destroyers, four corvettes, two anti-aircraft ships, three rescue vessels and even two submarines.

In addition the convoy would be shadowed by a mixed Royal Navy/US Navy group of four cruisers and three destroyers. Also in the area would be a battle group including two battleships, an aircraft carrier, two cruisers and 14 destroyers. The convoy was to be escorted as far as Bear Island by surface warships and thereafter the onus would fall mainly on the British submarines to provide cover. The reason for

Kapitänleutnant Joachim Schepke (1912–1941) wearing his Knights Cross with Oakleaves, which was awarded in December 1940. The same year he published a book entitled *U-boat Fahrer von heute* ('U-boat men of today') describing life on board a U-boat and illustrated with his own paintings. U-100 was his third command when he was killed in action.

such a heavy warship presence was the proximity of German Navy bases in Norway to the convoy route. A number of German heavy units including the battleship *Tirpitz* were known to be lurking in these bases and might well be tempted to attack such a large and important convoy.

The first contact between U-boats and the convoy was made on 1 July, but the submarines were driven off by the escorts. An attack by German aircraft later that day was also successfully driven off. It was not until 4 July that the first casualty occurred when German aircraft succeeded in damaging one ship, which would later be sunk by U-457. U-334 also succeeded in sinking a US transport ship on this same day.

Despite these losses, the damage to the convoy had so far been relatively light. Unfortunately confusion reigned within British naval command as to whether or not a German task force including *Tirpitz* had sailed to intercept the convoy. Despite all evidence to the contrary, Admiral Sir Dudley Pound insisted that the Germans were about to attack and at 2215hrs on 4 July ordered the cruiser force and other escorts withdrawn and the convoy to scatter. PQ17 had gone from a relatively safe, well-defended convoy to a scattered group of individual ships, defenceless and at the mercy of the enemy.

Early on 5 July, U-88 attacked and sank two US-registered freighters and U-456 another. Two British merchants were sunk by U-703 and a third by U-334. On 6 July U-255 sank another US-registered vessel and added a further vessel to her score on the following day. U-457 and U-355 both sank one ship each on 7 July, US and British victims respectively. On the following day, U-255 added yet another to her score. A two-day respite followed before U-251 and U-376 each sank merchants. The final victim, a Dutch registered vessel, was added to the score of U-255 on 13 July.

PERISCOPE VIEW

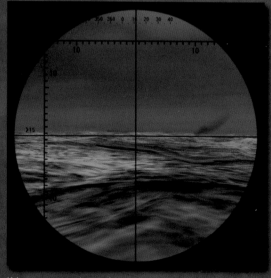

U-boat commander positions his vessel at a right angle to the merchant ship where it presents the biggest target.

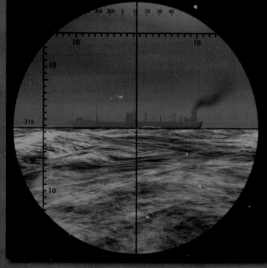

Rohr Eins – Los! Tube One – Fire!

In all, 16 merchantmen were sunk by U-boats, seven of them after first being damaged by German aircraft. Eight more were sunk by aircraft action alone. Over 3,700 vehicles including hundreds of tanks, and over 200 aircraft were lost on the merchantmen that had been sunk, to say nothing of the over 150 merchant seamen who lost their lives. Whilst some of these ships may well have been lost even if the convoy had not scattered, the carnage which resulted would almost certainly have been avoided.

In the event, *Tirpitz* and other German warships did sortie from their bases on 5 July, after PQ 17 had already scattered, but when they became aware of the possible presence of Allied warships in the area, and aware that the convoy had already been decimated, returned to their bases later the same day. The entire battle is indicative of how crucial the convoy system was to keeping the vital lifeline open between Great Britain and her Allies. Scattering a convoy when U-boats were circling like a group of hungry predators was a recipe for disaster.

The U-boats fared reasonably well at the start of 1943. On 20 February, convoy ON166, a fast east-bound convoy to the USA was intercepted by U-604. As more U-boats gathered they found themselves faced with a vigorous escorting force. Although two ships were sunk, it was only with the loss of one U-boat, with another damaged and the remainder of the gathering pack driven off.

On the night of 21 February an attack by U-91 saw two merchantmen torpedoed but with another U-boat missing believed destroyed.

The escorts succeeded in keeping the U-boats at bay during daylight on 22 February but a night attack resulted in three more ships being sunk. U-606 however, was rammed and damaged by an escort during this action and forced to withdraw. One small vessel which had fallen behind the convoy to pick up survivors was itself torpedoed and sunk.

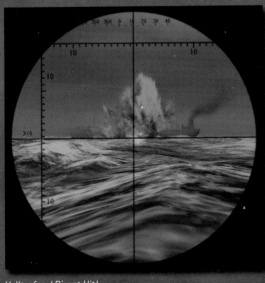

Volltrefeer! Direct Hit!

Having detected the sound of slow moving ships which indicated merchant vessels, the U-boat is at periscope depth and the first visual evidence of the enemy is seen. It takes some time to manoeuvre the boat into an ideal firing position and the crew keep a look out for escorts which may appear at any time. The commander calculates the firing angle allowing for the speed of the torpedo, the distance it has to cover and the position of the enemy, firing ahead of the enemy vessel so that the torpedo reaches the spot at the same time as the target. Depending on the target, either a single torpedo or a "spread" would be fired.

In many cases, the U-Boat would dive immediately after firing its torpedo, seeking the relative safety of greater depth. In any case, vision would not necessarily be required to confirm a hit – the detonation of the torpedo against the target would tell all.

The troopship USS *Neville* as part of an east-bound convoy in 1942. Troopships were particularly attractive targets for U-boats, their sinking resulting in the loss not only of a valuable ship, but much-needed manpower on the front line. (National Archives)

The following day saw more determined attacks by the Wolfpack with seven ships being sunk in daylight and night attacks as the escorts tried to fend off U-boat attacks whilst doing their best to recover survivors from sunken merchant ships. The arrival of air cover and more escorts on 24 February saw the U-boat successes dwindle with only one further merchant sunk, and on the morning of 25 February the U-boats finally broke off the engagement. A total of 14 merchant ships totalling 88,000 tons had been lost, but the nineteen U-boats involved, from two separate Wolfpacks, had four of their own lost or damaged.

German cipher experts had cracked the British naval codes allowing a Wolfpack of 39 U-boats to be vectored onto the positions of eastward bound convoys SC 122 and HX 229. Some 21 merchant ships totalling over 140,000 tons were sunk for the loss of just three U-boats. However, such successes were to become increasingly rare and by the middle of 1943, U-boat successes against Allied convoys had dwindled alarmingly. Indeed, in the spring of that year, two convoys managed to cross safely without losing a single ship despite attacks by U-boats, but in contrast six U-boats were destroyed by escort forces. In the three month period between April and July 1943, well over a hundred U-boats were lost to enemy action.

One of the last major successes for the U-boats came in the spring of 1943 when slow westbound convoy ONS 5 was intercepted by U-650 on 28 April. Three other U-boats quickly reached the scene but their attempts to attack the convoy during the night came to nothing and two of them were so heavily damaged by attacks from the escorts that they were forced to break off and return to base. Over the next two days one merchant vessel was sunk as the U-boats struggled against both determined escort forces and worsening weather conditions. Contact with the convoy was lost during the storms and the convoy scattered. The attackers were then diverted towards another convoy, SC 128. Fortunately for the Allies, this convoy SC 128 was able to completely avoid the U-boats hunting it, but unfortunately for ONS 5, now re-formed, ran into the new patrol line set up to intercept SC 128. During the night of 3 May, one ship from ONS 5 was sunk, but again the U-boats took a hammering from the escorts with three of their number forced to withdraw from the battle, seriously damaged.

Eventually, four U-boats, U-707, U-628, U-258 and U-264 were able to penetrate the escort screen and between them sink five merchant ships. The attack continued during the next day, with four more ships sunk but only at the cost of one U-boat destroyed and another damaged. By the evening of that day, at least 15 U-boats were in contact with the convoy but it was aided by the appearance of a large fogbank which gave the ships some degree of cover. Throughout that night, well over twenty separate attacks were made by the U-boat but none succeeded. Instead, four more U-boats were detected on the surface by Radar and sunk by the convoy's escorts. The arrival of a powerful support group of escorts during the following morning resulted in two more U-boats being destroyed, forcing the Germans to call off the attack.

A final tally of 12 ships totalling around 62,000 tons had been sunk, but only at the tremendous cost of six U-boats destroyed and a further seven badly damaged. This would be the last time so many ships would be lost from a single convoy, but the cost to the Germans in U-boats destroyed was greater than they could afford and on 23 May 1943, Grossadmiral Dönitz suspended operations in the North Atlantic. Over 360 U-boat crewmen were lost, one of whom was Dönitz's own son.

But operations persisted in other regions of the Atlantic with continued high losses on both sides. On 17 October 1943, U-841 was operating east of Cape Farewell, attempting to close with other boats forming the *Schlieffen* Wolfpack, which had been ordered to attack convoy ONS 20. This U-boat was detected by the Frigate HMS *Byard* (a Buckley Class DE) and suffered heavy depth charging. She was forced to the

The final moments of Buckley Class DE USS *Fiske* as she rolls to port, her back broken, after being torpedoed by U-804 on 2 August 1944.

A Mechanikermaat is shown attaching clamped bands to a torpedo whilst his crewmate reads on his bunk indicative of how every available inch was utilized on board. (Royal Naval Submarine Museum)

surface where the DE engaged her with gunfire causing further serious damage. It is reported that the die-hard U-boat captain actually resorted to firing at the DE with his pistol whilst his men prepared to scuttle. Although 27 of the U-boat crew were rescued, the remainder, including the commander, were lost with their boat.

In the latter stages of the war the Allies continued to refine their anti-submarine warfare tactics. Building upon the success of the convoy system and the aggressive tactics that ASDIC and Radar developments encouraged, the Allies increasingly needed to ensure that convoys were not left open to attack whilst its escorts pursued other U-boats. As a result, Convoy Support Groups were established. These fast warships would pursue any U-boats detected, whilst leaving the regular escorts with the convoy to maintain a defensive cover. By 1944 Support Groups were at the height of their success. One of each group would follow the last noted course of a detected U-boat, at speed, pinging the U-boat with ASDIC. The remainder would follow at much slower speeds and not using their own ASDIC but being fed information on the U-boat's position by the lead escort. The tactic worked and one group, the 2nd Support Group consisting of six escorts under the command of Captain Johnny Walker destroyed six U-boats in just three weeks.

U-boat losses had become increasingly unsustainable and in the first quarter of 1944 alone, 54 U-boats were sunk. One such victim was U-66. A highly successful Type IXC, she was on her tenth and last patrol having sunk four merchant ships in the South Atlantic when, on 19 April 1944, a radio signal from her was detected and another on 1 May. Aware that a U-boat was operating in the area, an escort group including an aircraft carrier had been maintaining heavy air surveillance, which had prevented the U-boat from surfacing to charge her batteries.

Eventually on 5 May the U-boat was forced to surface to recharge her batteries and was immediately detected by Allied Radar. An aircraft was launched to guide one of the escort group's DEs, USS *Buckley* to the U-boat's position. As soon as the U-boat was in range, the DE opened fire, hitting her conning tower. The U-boat, its batteries almost flat, was unable to dive and returned fire with her deck gun. *Buckley* rapidly closed on the U-boat and rammed her. A number of German sailors who had been on the conning tower jumped on to the forecastle of the DE and hand-to-hand fighting ensued before the German sailors were subdued. American sailors meanwhile lobbed grenades into the open conning tower hatch of the U-boat. *Buckley* then reversed, pulling away from the U-boat which continued to fire, scoring hits on the escort. Eventually, after further direct hits from *Buckley's* 3-in. gun the submarine succumbed and sank, with *Buckley* rescuing 36 of the U-boat's crew. Thus ended one of the war's most unusual engagements where armed U-boat crewmen effectively boarded a US escort.

Buckley and her crew received an official commendation for their achievement. The citation reported her crew repelling the enemy boarders with "guns fists and even coffee cups". The episode is also indicative of the growing importance of aircraft in the battle against U-boats. Used in conjunction with the DE, few U-boats stood a chance of escaping attack.

On 18 November 1944, U-775 left Bergen for operations around the British coast. Her patrol area was between Cape Wrath and the Pentland Firth to the north of Scotland. On 6 December 1944, she spotted an enemy warship and went into the attack, hitting the Captain Class frigate HMS *Bullen*, which sank with the loss of 71 of her crew. The U-boat had stirred up a hornet's nest however, and for the next 14 hours she was tracked by frigates HMS *Loch Insh* and HMS *Goodall* as well as a Sunderland flying boat. U-775 escaped, but the forces hunting her spotted another U-boat snorkelling. This new boat was U-297. She dived but was subjected to a ferocious depth charge attack and destroyed with all hands. The hunters had now

Torpedomen placing a depth charge into position for dropping from the stern of the destroyer HMS *Eskimo* just out of harbour (possibly Hvalfjord) after a U-boat hunt in the Atlantic. Seldom were the ships in harbour long enough for any kind of relaxation. Overhauling and cleaning torpedoes and depth charges, checking gyroscopes, stripping guns, and changing ammunition, were just some of the tasks that needed to be done. (IWM A7414)

HMS *Viscount*'s depth charge party bringing up fresh charges after an attack on a U-boat so they can be fitted to the stern-mounted racks. (IWM A 13370)

become the hunted as the Allies' sheer weight of numbers, ability to restock and maintain the merchant and escort fleets, technological edge and the effective use of the DE/frigate reaped its grim harvest of U-boats.

But it was not always an entirely unequal duel between U-boats and the DEs. When engaged in one-on-one actions, aided by the element of surprise, the U-boats could enjoy incredible success even as late as the closing months of 1944. On 26 November of that year, a newly commissioned Type VII U-boat, U-486, left Egersund in Norway under the command of Oberleutnant zur See Gerhard Meyer to attack Allied shipping in the English Channel. On 18 December she sank the *Silverlaurel* off Plymouth and on 21 December, she torpedoed the troop transport *Leopoldville* near Cherbourg, carrying over 2,200 troops. Although some troops were evacuated from the sinking troop carrier over 800 were lost when it finally sank. Evading the escorts hunting her, U-486 remained in the area and on 26 December torpedoed and sank the Captain Class frigate HMS *Capel* and only minutes later hit the frigate HMS *Affleck* with another torpedo. Although the latter vessel did not sink, and was towed into port, she was damaged beyond repair. It was, however, to be the only successful patrol for U-486. On leaving port on her next patrol she developed a fault and turned about, running on the surface she was spotted by a British submarine and torpedoed. She was lost with all hands.

In the last weeks of the war, actions between U-boats and DEs generally could have only one possible conclusion as the following examples show. U-248 left Trondheim on 3 December 1944 and by early January was on weather-reporting duty in the North Atlantic. On 4 January she was located by the Buckley Class DE

USS *Hubbard* but the warship was unable to pin down her exact location. The same group of escorts located her again on 18 December north of the Azores and she was subjected to a concerted attack by *Varian*, *Otter*, *Hubbard* and *Hayter* and was sunk with all hands.

On 6 February 1945, U-399 was operating in the Western Approaches when she encountered Convoy TBC 103 near Eddystone on 21 March. She torpedoed and damaged the *James Eagan Layne*. Five days later she encountered Convoy BTC 108 which she attacked, sinking the *Pacific*. Her success was short lived, however, and minutes later she was detected by the DE HMS *Duckworth* and subjected to heavy depth-charge attacks and was sunk with all hands.

On 6 January 1945, U-480 had departed Trondheim for the waters of the British coast. By latter part of the month she had reached the Western Approaches where she attacked Convoy BTC 78 and sank the *Oriskany*. A search for the submarine began and on 24 January she was located by two escorts, the Captain Class DEs HMS *Duckworth* and HMS *Rowley* and sunk with all hands.

In March 1945 U-546 was patrolling south of Cape Farewell when she was spotted by a US aircraft and the US Navy. Alerted to the German presence, surface warships were despatched to locate and destroy her. It initially seemed as if the hunters would become the hunted, however, as the Edsall Class DE USS *Frederick C Davis* was torpedoed and sunk by the U-boat on arrival at the scene. Nevertheless, more DEs quickly gathered and U-546 was detected by USS *Flaherty*, depth charged and heavily damaged. Forced to the surface the U-boat launched a torpedo at the DE but missed. By now, U-546 was under attack by a total of no fewer than eight DEs, the *Hubbard*, *Flaherty*, *Varian*, *Pillsbury*, *Chatelein*, *Neunzer*, *Janssen* and *Keith*. In the face of such overwhelming numbers her fate was sealed. Indeed, the war itself was over less than two months later. The costliest campaign of the entire conflict – the Battle of the Atlantic – was at an end.

Dönitz's plan for submarine warfare against Great Britain estimated that the destruction of around 800,000 tons of shipping per month would eventually bring the British to their knees. In fact by 1942, the losses of 650,000 tons of shipping per month was already having a crippling effect on the British. However, the tide effectively turned with the sustained use of the convoy system in the face of such appalling losses and the increasing ability to replace lost merchant vessels and the effective use of anti-submarine tactics and weaponry, not least of all, the Destroyer Escort.

Captain Frederic John Walker, DSO and three Bars, was an officer of the Royal Navy and the most successful anti-submarine commander during the Battle of the Atlantic. He was popularly known as 'Johnnie' Walker, presumably after the whisky. His son, Timothy, was killed when the submarine HMS *Parthian* was lost in August 1943, an event that strengthened his resolve to secure victory for the Allies. Walker suffered a cerebral thrombosis on 7 July 1944 and died two days later, his death ultimately attributed to overwork and exhaustion. (IWM A-21313)

STATISTICAL ANALYSIS

THE CONVOY

Well over 200 different convoy designations were used during World War II. The two or three-letter prefix indicated the route with a numerical suffix denoting the convoy number. The prime target routes for the U-boats included:

    HX – From Halifax, Nova Scotia to the UK

    CU – Caribbean to UK (oil tankers)

    SL – Sierra Leone to UK

    PQ – From Reykjavik, Iceland, to Murmansk in the Soviet Union

    SC – From Sydney, Australia to the UK

    OB – UK to North America

    ON – UK to North America (Fast)

    ONS – UK to North America (Slow)

    OS – UK to Sierra Leone

    QP – Russia to Iceland

Clearly, UK-bound convoys laden with essential war supplies were particularly important targets for the U-boats, depriving Britain of not only ships but much needed supplies. Even those west-bound empty merchants sailing back across the Atlantic were important targets however, especially in the early part of the war whilst merchant losses were outstripping new builds.

The most successful U-boats

Boat	Type	Ships sunk	Approx. tonnage
U-48	VIIB	54	320,400
U-103	IXB	45	238,400
U-99	VIIB	35	238,300
U-124	IXB	48	224,000
U-107	IXB	38	212,800
U-47	VIIB	32	211,400
U-123	IXB	41	209,800
U-68	IXC	33	198,000
U-66	IXC	33	197,300

Each boat during its career had more than one commander. These totals refer to the tonnages sunk by the boat, not any specific commander. Of all of these boats, U-103 and U-123 were decommissioned in 1944 and U-48 scuttled in 1945. All of the others were lost to enemy action.

U-Boat construction/losses

	New Boats	Lost	Overall Strength
1939	6	9	54
1940	54	25	83
1941	202	35	250
1942	238	85	403
1943	290	241	452
1944	230	254	428
1945	93	172	349

A Type VII moving at speed on the surface. Although far more cramped and uncomfortable than the larger Type IX, the Type VII could dive faster and many crewmen felt that the greater potential for a successful escape from the enemy made the lack of comfort worthwhile. (Author's collection)

Merchant shipping losses from Atlantic convoys		
	Shipping sunk (Approx)	Tonnage (approx)
1939	147	509,300
1940	513	2,435,600
1941	431	2,224,900
1942	1,000	5,385,700
1943	310	1,860,200
1944	61	313,700
1945	54	231,000

In addition 159 merchant ships totalling 585,300 tons were sunk by U-boats in the Mediterranean, and 158 ships totalling 940,400 tons in the Indian and Pacific Oceans. Smaller numbers were also sunk in the Baltic and Black seas.

In all, around 2,900 ships were sunk by U-boat action during World War II, totalling in the region of 14 million tons.

Escort losses						
	Destroyers	DE/frigates	Sloops	Corvettes	Others	Total
1939	0	0	0	0	6	6
1940	4	0	2	0	0	6
1941	6	0	1	6	5	18
1942	15	0	3	4	19	41
1943	11	3	0	3	6	23
1944	6	12	4	4	6	32
1945	0	3	3	4	5	15

Of the total of 141 escort vessels lost in combat with U-boats, 19 were lost by the US Navy, the bulk of the remainder being vessels of the Royal and Commonwealth navies, and ships of Allied nations such the Free French and Polish navies operating from British ports.

CONCLUSION

In World War I, the introduction of the convoy system had played a major role in preventing the U-boats from strangling Britain's sea lanes. In World War II, the Kriegsmarine's U-boats had initially scored some dramatic successes despite their main submarine model, the Type VII, being basically an improved version of the Type UBIII of World War I. Before long, however, the reintroduction of the convoy system coupled with improved anti-submarine warfare equipment such as ASDIC and Radar, highly effective weapons such as the Hedgehog mortar and the availability of effective airborne anti-submarine weaponry, meant that the U-Bootwaffe was always struggling to devise new counter-measures. The most devastating blow of all however, was the Allied cracking of the Enigma codes which often allowed the Allies full knowledge of German plans.

Only the development of advanced submarine models such as the Type XXI and Type XXIII gave the Germans vessels which would have stood a chance of combating and overwhelming Allied superiority on the sea and in the air and both types (although the Type XXI was made in large numbers) saw too little service, too late to effect the outcome of the war.

In the early part of World War II, the numbers of Allied merchantmen sunk by U-boats was greater than Britain's capacity to build new ships. Had the USA not entered the war, despite the availability of Asdic, Radar and the cracking of the Enigma codes, prospects for Britain would have been bleak indeed.

The entry of the USA into the war brought not just significant numbers of escort warships with which the convoys could be protected, but perhaps even more significantly, the industrial capacity to mass-manufacture cargo ships with the arrival of Henry Kaiser's famed Liberty ships. The Allies were now capable of building merchant vessels at a far faster rate than the U-boats could sink them. Over 2,700

Ordinary Seaman P. S. Buckingham of Norwich keeping a record of U-boat kills on the side of the wheelhouse on board HMS *Hesperus* whilst docked at Liverpool. (IWM A 20897)

Liberty Ships were built between 1941 and 1945. The average construction time for these ships was just 42 days and the record set, with the construction of the SS *Robert E Peary,* saw the ship launched (but not fitted out or completed) just over 4 days from the day the keel was laid!

During the life of the U-Bootwaffe, 1,131 boats had entered service. Of these, 863 took part in active war patrols, from which 754 were sunk, an attrition rate of 87%. Of the 754 boats which were sunk, 458 were lost in action in the Atlantic. Although a few fortunate survivors from sunken U-boats were picked up, of the 39,000 men who served, some 28,730 or just over 73%, were killed in action.

It is estimated that around 75,000 merchant seamen had their ships sunk by U-boats. Many were rescued, but around 32,000 of them died. A considerable number of Royal Navy personnel were also lost on escorts sunk by U-boats.

Despite the hunters of the first half of the war having become the hunted, the psychological as well as physical effects of the U-boat war were sufficient for Winston Churchill to declare, after victory had been won, 'The only thing that ever really frightened me during the war was the U-boat peril'.

Interestingly, post-World War II, it is the submarine and its nemesis, the destroyers and frigates, which have become the mainstay of naval power. The huge battleships of World War II have been consigned to history. Submarines are now vast warships of up to 50,000 tons, often nuclear powered and with destructive power unimaginable in the 1940s. The modern destroyers and frigates, usually armed with guided missiles will often have destructive power surpassing that of the battleships of old and anti-submarine warfare equipment including ASW helicopters, beyond the wildest dreams of the escort crews of the Battle of the Atlantic.

FURTHER READING

Haskell, Winthrop A. *Shadows on the Horizon* (London, Chatham Publishing 1998)

Kaplan, Philip and Currie, Jack, *Wolfpack* (London; Aurum Press Ltd 1997)

Kaplan, Philip and Currie, Jack, *Convoy* (London; Aurum Press Ltd 1998)

Kurowski, Franz, *Die Träger des Ritterkreuzes des Eisernen Kreuzes der U-Bootwaffe 1939-5.* (Friedberg; Podzun Pallas Verlag 1987)

Mallmann-Showell, Jak P., *U-Boats under the Swastika* (Surrey; Ian Allan 1998)

Mallmann-Showell, Jak P., *U-Boats in Camera* (Stroud; Sutton Publishing 1999)

Miller, David, *U-Boats; The Illustrated History of the Raiders of the Deep* (Limpsfield; Pegasus Publishing Ltd 1999)

Paterson, Lawrence, *U-boat War Patrol: The Hidden Photographic Diary of U564* (Annapolis, Naval Institute Press 2004)

Rössler, Eberhard, *The U-Boat; The evolution and technical history of German submarines* (London; Arms & Armour Press 1981)

Sharpe, Peter, *U-Boat Fact File* (Leicester; Midland Publishing Limited 1998)

Stern, Robert C, *Type VII U-Boats* (London; Arms & Armour Press 1991)

Tarrant, V. E., *U-Boat Offensive 1914-1945* (Annapolis 1989)

Taylor, J.C., *German Warships of World War Two* (London; Ian Allan 1966)

Williams, Andrew, *The Battle of the Atlantic* (BBC Publications, London, 2002)

Wynn, Kenneth, *U-Boat Operations of the Second World War Vol 1* (London; Chatham Publishing 1997)

Wynn, Kenneth, *U-Boat Operations of the Second World War Vol 2* (London; Chatham Publishing 1998)

bbc.co.uk/ww2peopleswar an online archive of wartime memories contributed by members of the public and gathered by the BBC.

INDEX